God Lives

The Loving Light Books Series

Also by Liane Rich

Loving Light

Book 12

God Lives

Liane Rich

The information contained in this book is not intended as a substitute
for professional medical advice. Neither the publisher nor the author is
engaged in rendering professional advice to the reader. The remedies
and suggestions in this book should not be taken, or construed, as
standard medical diagnosis, prescription or treatment. For any medical
issue or illness consult a qualified physician.

ISBN 13: 978-1-878480-12-5
ISBN 10: 1-878480-12-X

Loving Light Books:
www.lovinglightbooks.com

Also Available at:
Amazon: www.amazon.com
Barnes & Noble: www.barnesandnoble.com

This is the perfect plan! This is creation at its finest. This is light spreading through everything that is. This is the grand awakening and this is the whole coming together with itself. This is the return of God to God.

The information in this series is not necessarily meant to be taken literally. It is meant to *shift* your consciousness....

Foreword

Anyone immersed in the vast body of new metaphysical knowledge is aware of the virtual symphony of voices from channeled sources throughout the world – inspirational voices that may be artistic, poetic, philosophical, religious, or scientific. And now, out of these myriad New Age voices, comes a series of books by God, channeled through Liane, revealing the frank truth in all its glory and wonder, telling us how to cleanse our bodies, gain access to our subconscious minds, clear our other selves and march back to who we are – God.

In God's books you will be introduced to a loving, powerful, gripping, exciting, and often humorous voice that reaches out and speaks ever so personally to the individual reader. As the reader's interest deepens, invariably an intimate relationship to this voice develops. It is a relationship that lasts forever, and I am quite certain I do mean forever.

Here is an accelerated program, a no-holds-barred course, where God guides us and loves us, and as needs be recommends books to us and even a movie or musical piece along the way. He (She) enters our lives and sees through our eyes, seeming to enjoy the ride as He guides us back to US, back to ALL. Here is a voice that is playful and informative, that is humorous and serious, that is gentle and powerfully divine. It is a voice that knows no barriers or restrictions, a straightforward and honest voice that caresses us when we need the warmth and pushes us when we are immobilized.

In today's New Age literature there is an avalanche of information from magnificent beings of light, information that possesses us and compels us to look at our fears and express our love. In this series of books by God, you will find truly powerful methods for making this transition from toxicity to purity, from density to light, from fear to love, and from the delusion of death to the awakening to full life. You will experience in these books the love and the power of God for it is your love to express and your power to behold. Rarely will you see more lucid steps for transformation. Read these beautiful words and rejoice in our period of awakening, our return to Home.

John Farrell, PhD., LCSW. – Psychologist, Clinical Social Worker, Senior Clinician Psychiatric Emergency Services, U.C. Davis Medical Center, Sacramento. John is also a retired Professor – California State University, Sacramento, in Health Sciences and Psychology.

God Lives

Introduction

*A*s you begin to transmute, you begin to draw out your old beliefs and your old programming. You literally begin to reprogram you to the extent that you feel pulled and stretched. You are taking all that you can take and what you are taking is light. Light enters you and dissipates the darkness. This does not feel good to you and you are shifting and changing your programming so fast that you may feel explored, as though you have given up every part of you and there is nothing left to give.

This is when you will begin your transformation from dark to light. This is when you will give up your hold on darkness. This is when you begin to switch from matter to light. You are beginning this process now and you are learning to surrender. Surrender is not easy for you, as you have always been taught to control. Now, however, I want you to surrender. I want you to give up control. I want you to go limp and to allow yourself to be molded into a new creation.

You are on the brink of discovering who you are and how to function as a "light being." Did you think this shift would be unnoticed by you? Did you think you would not feel it? This is the greatest gift you will ever receive and, once you have moved through it, you will be so "light" you will astound yourself with the fluidity of your life and your path. You will begin to float through life as you float through death. You will begin to *know* without being told. You will begin to see without being guided. You will become an ascended being living in a multidimensional world. You will have the best of all worlds and you will literally walk with God at your side. You will become God and know who you are.

Ascension is here. This is a time of great expansion and transformation. Information is being received as never before. This is it. The time is now. You are God and you are going to start acting like you are. You have gone far and wide in your search for your true identity. Everyone is trying to find themselves and they are right inside where they have been dormant for eons. Now is the awakening, now is the rising up period. This will be good to see. You are in a place that was created long ago and it has been changed to light just by your willingness to enter it. You may release and change the past by seeing it again through the emotional body and allowing the "feelings" to move. They are stuck and they are sticking you. You are being prepared for your future by letting go of your past.

Your past is not important in that it can, and will, be replaced. In looking at it differently, with a greater perspective, you are able to set the past free and therefore create a new present moment. Once movement begins in the emotional body, it is impossible to hold you down. You are moving and reshaping your future by going into your past in such an emotionally charged fashion. This shows you how you *thought* it was, so that *now* in the present moment you may attach a new clearer vision to it. This will move the entire situation out of judgment against self and into, "Oh, I see how and why I have withheld my good all my life."

This is the gift! When you re-experience the original pain and you attach new thought to it, it then may become something other than pain. Anything may transmute or transform into something new and lighter. This is how you go up! One situation at a time, so do not judge your situation.

For the most part, you are learning to become light. You are learning to expand and take on light. It is not so difficult as it is uncomfortable for you. It is new to you and you do not like change. This change, however, will become one of the greatest gifts you will ever give. You are now giving to the self. And what are you giving yourself? You are giving yourself you. You are the gift. You are becoming you and you are full of light. Light is brilliance and brilliance is intelligence. You are wisdom and intelligence and light.

This is the most glorious time for you. You of the "A" team are beginning your descent down into you in order to rise up out of you. You are rising up out of yourself and learning to be above what you have always been a part of. You are moving up above this particular dimension. You are moving up *within* your own self to a new level of vibration. You will see with new eyes and you will know as you have never known before.

As you begin to move up this level of vibratory frequency you will find that things no longer affect you as they once did. You will no longer suffer pangs of loneliness and you will no longer feel the need to attach to others for security. You will be floating in your own light. You will know your own ability to create good. You will rise above pettiness into the realms of expanded knowing. You will find yourself totally free to move in any direction whatsoever. This will be you, free-floating in your own light. Light is God force and light is love. Love is vibrant and love is very powerful. Light is truth and love is wisdom and acceptance of all truth.

So; as you become this new ascended light being, you will begin to feel the shift within. It will be subtle at first and then it will grow. You will begin to lose interest in goal setting and decision making. It will become much more joyful to simply allow your light to create for you while you sit back and watch. This is your new role. You are observer. You are no longer in control; you are now in the audience watching your light create your future. "Whatever will be will be." You are now taking a backseat to the real driver who is God. You were created for God to use and now God is reclaiming what is God's.

This is it. This is the end of the world as you know it. Darkness (ignorance) will no longer be allowed to reign. You are being put on notice. God lives! God is coming in and taking over. You will become God and you will be in heaven on earth. Only you know who you are and if you are ready. Only you know how you will allow this to occur for you. You are being entered by the light and the light will lift and inspire and set you free! You are light and you are taking on more of what you are. You are God and you are taking on more of what you are. You are growing in you. You are conceiving God into matter.

You have come to such an extended use of creativeness. You have come full circle and gone from light to dark and back to the light. God is becoming in the darkest corners of creation. Light is entering all matter to expose it to truth and love. Fear is being transformed into love. Darkness is dissolving into light, and fear will no longer rule. Once light enters, truth will prevail and the lie will be exposed for all to see. This is the process you are going through. This is the stretching you feel. Growth! God is growing in you! You are it. You are creating God right now!

꧁꧂

You are now in the process of extending your life. The more light you take on, or in, the greater your expansion of life becomes. You will live and deal with all life with an ease and a gracefulness that is all new to you. You will no longer struggle to survive and you will no longer feel the need to fight, argue, push, win or beat anyone in any way. You will simply allow all to occur and you will move gracefully and easily through life.

You are now coming to a point in creation that is transition. The turning point is here and many will begin to feel the changes occurring in their lives. They will slip into change as you will, or they will fight every step of the way. Free will allows you to choose and many will choose struggle. Allow them to be and allow them to use what they will to create their personal reality. You are you and you are in charge of your reality and not how everyone else tries to live, or not live, according to their own independent beliefs. One of the easiest ways to get along is to "live and let live." This is ease and grace. Know what you know, and simply remember that what you know is simply your *truth* out of billions of ideas of truth available. What you know is also subjective to where you are right now and how much you can be told without freaking out.

You are all simply learning to grow and you are not *in* another's body, so you must concentrate your growth from within your own body and no longer project your growing patterns onto another. It is very important to realize that all cells within the master body of cells are learning to be individual expressions of the same force. It is as though some of you are bluebells and some are daisies and others are roses. I do not expect a bluebell to tell a rose how it should look or act. A rose knows, as all information is encoded in the rose in its cellular structure. All flowers know how to look and respond to light. It is not necessary to push a bloom open. It will naturally open when enough light has rested on it.

This is the nature of creation and it is no longer necessary to push open buds to see their splendor before they are ready to naturally display themselves. You are each learning to be who and what you are now in the process of becoming, and it is most important to allow you the time that is necessary for you to discover what you are and how you will open to the light. You are all in the process of opening in your own way and for your own desired effect. Do not push at the others to be better or different than they now are. They may be doing exactly what is necessary to get them to where they are going. You are trying to fix you by fixing everyone outside of you. Please remember that you are inside of you!

***

This is the beginning of a new era. Everything will shift and you will, more than likely, feel the shift within. How can you not? You are the world. You are creator and you are creation. If God is moving, you are moving. You are gaining momentum and you are coming alive and awake. You are speeding into you. You are light entering darkness and you are God entering matter.

This three-dimensional world, as you know it, is beginning to move. You are shifting into the fourth dimension and moving up to that vibration. This is being done now in order to speed up information and intelligence. Information will allow you to see from a greater perspective and it will lead you to awareness. You are beginning to learn that you are more than what you see and that what you see is nothing compared to what actually is here.

You are learning by your own willingness to rise. You want help. You want more. You have asked repeatedly for assistance and assistance is at hand for those who wish it. It is simply a matter of trust. Can you trust? How great is your trust and your belief that you are moving in the best possible direction? It is not always easy to trust. You have much that leads you astray and you have much that teaches you to not trust your own choices. After all, you grew up being told what you could and could not do. Mostly you were told what you could not do, as a child will always want to run and play with no thought of danger.

So, now you are this adult and you wish to make good choices for yourself, yet you have this child in you who knows from experience that nothing you ever want to do is right. This is how you are teaching yourself to take good care of yourself now, as an adult. You are going beyond and rising above these childhood beliefs. You are becoming whole by gathering to you all parts of you. You are taking on your own fears and demons. Those parts of you who do not trust are coming into you to center and be accepted. In accepting all parts of you with understanding, you now create love. Love is self-fulfilling. You are love and in accepting all parts of you, you accept love

This is a very good time for you. It feels confusing and you are afraid of change, but it is best. Trust that you are being guided and trust that you will know who you are and how you are rising. You are being transformed into a fearless being and this means that your fears must be met and faced for what they are. All fear is illusion and is attached to an event from past childhood or past-life. Sometimes a fear is simply *learned* and handed down. With this in mind, I wish you to remember that you are free to make your own choices now. You are not a child being programmed to not do this or that for fear of hurt or punishment. God does not punish you and you are learning to not punish you.

For the first time it is safe to not punish you. You have no more rules saying you are bad. You have no reason to punish you. You may let go of self-punishment and, as you do, your life will improve and begin to flow. Struggle will become a thing of the past. All struggle is actually inner turmoil being projected outward. Struggle ends when you simply accept with understanding and allow yourself to be your creator without judging what you create. It is a matter of trust. Trust you!

As you begin to know more of you, you will begin to allow for greater confusion. You are allowing you to re-create you and you will find that in the rebirthing, or dying off of some parts and rejuvenation of others, you will create a sense of right and wrong or "this is good/this is not good." This will come as you reject what you no longer wish to keep and you save what you like. It is like you are reconstructing you from the inside out... literally.

You are in the process of transmuting from one form to another and from one way of seeing life to another. This transformation will take you into some areas that may be quite frightening for you. Say you have a fear of always being alone. This fear may be reinforced or made bigger until you can move the feelings that are trapped behind this fear. Once the feelings begin to move, you are in a position to feel new feelings regarding aloneness. After all, if fear is blocking an emotional event in your life, you may not fully appreciate all sides of said event.

You may not enjoy being alone and yet crave for aloneness. In such cases you are trapped in your fear of loneliness. You are afraid to be alone and you are afraid to not be alone. You have blocked the pathways to the event itself. Judgment has frozen your emotions in position and so you have fear of being alone and fear of not being alone. Do you ever wonder why you destroy your relationships and then sit in your aloneness and say, "Why don't I have anyone?" It is all because your emotional track is plugged up with fear. You have fear regarding loneliness which is the same energy as being fulfilled in a relationship. When you are fulfilled you are never lonely and when you are lonely you are never fulfilled.

The trick is to get this emotional energy up and moving. As emotions begin to move, you may *feel* your emotions and respond emotionally. You may be sad, happy, crying, frowning – any number of emotional expressive behaviors. You may wish to not feel all that you are, however, it will *release* the fear that is blocking the pathway to your fulfillment. Look at it this way. You are being cleaned out and your circuitry is being repaired and changed. You are being rewired to function at a much higher level and when you start to rewire your emotional body you tend to get rather *emotional.*

All that energy, which has been stuck for years,

begins to move and you begin to respond to emotional energy as you did when you were first learning how to *manage* your emotions. Only this time we are not going to shut down emotions in order to control them. We will instead begin to use this emotional energy to work within and to create. All energy is good and all energy serves a purpose. This is how you are going to learn to create in the future. You will use you to the extent you have never used you before. You are a powerhouse of energy, and as soon as we get you unblocked you will be in fine shape to create.

So; for those who are moving into the emotional body and feeling the emotions on such high levels, congratulations! You have begun to reverse some very basic energy blocks that will have a most profound effect on your future. You must remember that you are a living being, and a live being is a moving electric being. This is an energy adjustment that will allow you freedom to see fulfillment in your life.

*F*or the most part you are put in certain positions in life so that you may learn and grow. These positions are of your own choosing and usually you make the choice believing that it is a good choice for you. You choose and then you experience life. The problem comes only when you get stuck in your choices and are no longer flexible enough to move or change whatever is no longer good in your opinion.

You all do this. You all choose and then judge your choices and now you are becoming fearful of making any choice. You are so afraid of losing that you put yourself in situations that do not feel good to you. You trust only when it feels good and yet you are the one in control. You are the one who makes you stay whether it is what you want or not. You think you can change what you once made, into what you now want. I will tell you now that it is much easier to change you than it is to change someone else outside of you.

You are changeable and flexible only when you want to be. Usually if you can see some good in a situation you will move rather quickly. If you see financial security you will fly anywhere to gain it. This is due to the fact that you are afraid of your world. You are afraid of living in pain and you are afraid of never being any more than what you now are. How many of you have been able to say, day in and day out, "I am totally fulfilled and I need nothing more?" How do you think it would be to have no anxiety, no stress, no worry about life? Do you think it is possible? Yes, it is. You will get to this stage in your evolution.

Yes, it is a stage of evolution. It is a place you are headed towards. Heaven on earth is the birthright of those who choose to claim it. How do you claim it? You simply allow all to be good. You know with your heart that your situation is being created for a reason and then watch and see what you learn and how you change and grow. You are growing you know? Every minute of every day, every cell within you is completely changing. So how can you not change? How can you remain stuck when your body is moving and growing?

Grow with it, move out of your fears. Go into your fears with joy. Say, "Oh boy, here comes another opportunity for growth. Oh boy, here is what I have created to get me one step closer to my heaven on earth." You will find that all growth is good and it does not matter how you have chosen to grow as long as you do. You are in charge of you and you are doing what is best for you. You are working in total darkness and that is what frightens you. You do not have the ability at this time to see what the big picture is so you are afraid to take that next step. You constantly depend on others and I want you to begin to depend on you.

Trust you! Trust all that you are and that you became you for a reason. Trust that the part of you that knows all knows exactly what you are doing and even has a very good reason for doing it. You are all that is. You are the creator. You must begin to trust that you are. You must begin to accept all parts of you, even the parts you see as bad or hurtful. You have always been creator, but you will not accept that you are. You deny this part of you and you push it away. You are missing a big piece of you and the peace that is missing is God. You are now in a position to accept this part of yourself and to allow it to be you. You are God and God is in you and has always been. You deny what you are and when you deny part of you, that part becomes inaccessible to you.

You are the wondrous creator you so often praise

and yet you push that part of you back down into denial. You are keeping God in the dark. God must move forward and be recognized. God must be allowed to come into the light. The more you allow God to be you, the greater your ability to work from all parts of you in perfect harmony and balance. You are God. You are love. Act like you know who you are and you will become who you are that much sooner. You are not here to hide God. Let God out. He is trapped behind the darkness of your denial. Be afraid of nothing for *you* are everything!

⚜

*V*ery often you are afraid. You are afraid of your future, which indicates your low level of trust in you as your creator. You are most often not in control of how and what you create. You believe that you plan and put away for your future, but you do not always trust that this will be enough. Do not worry about your future. Live now! Live in this moment and allow the future to unfold as it is meant to.

As you begin to get yourself aligned and balanced, you will begin to create an entirely different future that will be in balance, as it came from balance. Like creates like – and so on and so forth. If it comes from light and love it is light and love. Your future will not be a product of a polluted past. Your past is now being re-created simply by seeing it differently and this leads to a newly created future that is based on clarity and understanding. The clearer and more aware you become, the greater clarity and awareness you will see in your future.

You are a product of now. You have allowed yourself to transcend time by moving into, and recollecting, old wounded parts of you. You are now healing by allowing these parts to rest and learn to integrate properly within your new awareness. As these parts continue to return, you will be healing more and more of you. How to get these parts back is easy enough. The simple "will" to know the self as whole and complete will draw all of you into you. You will magnetically pull all parts back to you by your desire for healing and your acceptance of light.

You are becoming what you have always been; only now you will know it. You are tuning in to who and what you have always been, be it programming, be it essence, be it God, be it body, be it mind. You have the ability to know and to touch all parts of you. You simply do not know that you do. You do not know that fear is not a part of your nature and you do not know that love is your nature.

I cannot even convince you now. You find it so difficult to relate to the fact that love is what you are, as you believe you are fear which leads you to judge yourself and stand in a position of low self-esteem. You are no longer going to create from low self-esteem. You are now becoming whole which will lead to love. With low self-esteem, it does not matter how good you do or how good something is, you will find fault, as low self-esteem creates fault finding. Now, when you switch over to high self-esteem, you begin to create and find only perfection, as high self-esteem looks for and always finds the very best. Low self-esteem will look for and always find the worst.

This is why I tell you to heal you and you will heal your entire world. You will see the perfection in the plan. You will come from intelligence and wisdom and an understanding that absolutely everything has a purpose. With this attitude you cannot possibly lose, as losing becomes a thing of the past. You know you are love and you know love grows and stretches and expands. It is so simple. As love takes over it spreads out like a giant blanket to cover the earth. Love goes forth, and divides, and separates, and spreads, and moves, and infiltrates, and permeates every part of creation, and, as each part is triggered to awaken, it will begin to move, and spread, and infiltrate, and so on.

This is the perfect plan! This is creation at its finest. This is light spreading through everything that is. This is the grand awakening and this is the whole coming together with itself. This is the return of God to God.

❧

For the most part you are in a stage of development which may affect your body in many ways. You may become very sluggish or you may become full of nervous energy. Either way it is energy moving and changing. Look at this entire situation like you are a car that has been turned over to a very good mechanic. When you are being adjusted it is difficult to drive you. You must be patient and allow all adjustments to occur. It is in this process that you become aligned and smooth functioning.

All adjustments that are now occurring are for your future on the road or highway to heaven. You are learning to ride a smooth path to your destination and you are learning to lighten your load for your own comfort. As you move through your clearing periods you will find that you *feel* lighter and more efficient. This, of course, is due to your new level of vibration that was allowed by simply shifting your comprehension up a notch. And how do we shift your comprehension up? We allow you to see how you are judging. And how do we allow you to see how you are judging? We put you in a situation that you wish to label bad, so that you may see through a higher awareness that you may also choose to name this same situation good. This is how we show you that you are in charge of creating what you see.

You comprehend what you see from where you are in your development. Each situation you are pushed into that feels uncomfortable is a testing ground to see if you will reach a high comprehensive vibration. You may stay low and decide the situation is not good, or you may switch to higher intelligence and see how the situation is simply a mirror placed in front of you to show you what you do to you. In this case you would then say, "Oh great, I am so glad I got to see how I am," and you would know that this is the part of you that the mechanic is now working on.

The areas that are most magnified to you at this time are the areas where you personally carry great fear. This fear is being cleared and you are being set free. You are each clearing and shifting up to higher gears in order to expand into the next dimension. You are moving up. I know this is not as glamorous as being lifted up in a big white cloud, but you will see and feel the benefits as you reach your own personal *peace* within. You see, all peace begins and ends with you. It is all within. And all war begins and ends with you. It too is created by you to keep you off balance.

You create struggle to keep you pushed and pulled at. It is the battle within that is reflected out into the world. You no longer need this type of stimulation to keep you charged. You are beginning to learn to run on light energy which takes no charge. The light simply floats and does not zing. The light penetrates and does not push. The light permeates and does not need to take over as it *is* already and will always *be*. Light is the truth. When you scrape away all the debris of matter that is encrusted on you, what you will find is your truest essence which is light. There is nothing else. Light is what you are and light is what you will always be.

You may cover light to lessen its brilliance or you may ignore light and pretend it is not there, but you cannot deny light as it is you and to deny you will eventually end you. You see, light does not end, however you have created a way to end you. So if you deny your basic essence you are pushing the light away and denying its right to be. In denying light, you deny you and in denying you, you lose you.

You will never find a better way to be you than simply to let you be. If you stop controlling you and judging you, you will eventually fall back into alignment with all creation. You will begin to be what you are. You are not a machine programmed to a schedule and you are not ignorant. You are the creator and the creator may do whatever the creator wishes. There is no one here to punish you for wrongdoing but you. You are caught up in right and wrong. The creator does not care. The creator will do what comes naturally. Trust your creator. Trust you!

So far you are beginning to see how maybe it is best to allow all to occur. Maybe it is best to let you be and allow all life to unfold as was meant. Now and then you find it difficult to believe that you are creating for you, as you begin to realize that creation is not always what you ordered. So why is it that you do not always get what you order? Could it be that what you order is not all that enlightening? Or could it be that what you order is best left alone so that you might receive another gift that is much, much bigger? Could it be that you are always exactly where you need to be and could it also be that you are being led to your right place? Could it be that the ego is leading you astray while the creator is seeking the path? Could it be that your orders get lost in the mail because the creator knows what will best serve you? And could it possibly be that absolutely everything is happening in perfect harmony, so why would you want to interfere?

I will tell you why you try to stop creation and change creation. You try to do so out of fear of loss of control. Control is a myth. You have no control, but guess what? The creator does and you know who the creator is? Right again. You are all that is. You are the creator and yet you deny the creator. You are darkness and light and you are struggling to know your balance. Balance will be found when you surrender. Give up and flow. Move with the flow of your life. Enjoy everything and know that it has purpose.

You may begin to enjoy life, by simply being who you are without fear of not being received. You are the only one who creates rejection simply by not receiving yourself. As you learn to receive yourself and be thankful to be you, you will see that everyone is thankful that you are you. You are but a reflection upon a reflection. You are flashing you signals to show you what you are and to allow you to see more of you.

You are the beginning and you are the end. You start and you finish and yet you turn around and complete again and again. You spin and whirl and take up all of time and space and yet you do not. You are everything and you are nothing and yet you may become anything at all. You are so wondrous. You may perform and create or you may sit back and observe as you perform and create. You are the actor and you are the audience. You unfold and separate into billions of lights and then you roll up into total darkness. You are everything and you are tricking you into believing that you are nothing with no great ability.

You will find that you are not only the most powerful, you are the most insignificant. You are light at its brightest and you are darkness at its darkest. You run from here to there and, in reality, there is no here or there. You have done it all and you have become it all. You are the creator and now it is the seventh day and you are about to rest.

※

You are one of the most unique individuals in that you have the ability to see whatever you wish to see simply by doing so. You no longer wish to see pain and ugliness and you no longer wish to be pain and ugliness. You may see the joy and the beauty in all simply by allowing it to be joy and beauty. The more you begin to see how you create your own reality by how you choose to view a situation from a perspective of good or bad, the more you will learn to tune in to the best perspective for you.

You may begin to want to see only joy, and therefore go back to our first three books and the story of the boy looking for his pony in a box of manure. You see, he had the right idea. Good is always there if you know that it is. You will always find your gifts if you simply look for gifts instead of looking for punishment. You are so programmed to "beware" that you have inadvertently programmed yourself to look for the danger or bad in everything.

I want you to begin to look for only the good. You will find good just as easily as you will find bad. You are good and everything that happens for you or for another is a gift. Someone getting shot in the back can be a gift of learning and even a gift of moving out of the material world. Just because this *thought* makes you uncomfortable does not change the fact that two souls had an agreement and came to earth and "acted out" that agreement. Maybe you are in on that agreement and they came in to act it out to help you get over your *fear* of death by shooting. As a matter of fact, maybe the whole shootout was done just for you, even though you don't remember asking to see this particular event so you could learn to clear your judgment concerning "bad" things happening.

So; does this shootout now become a good thing? Of course it does. It was asked for by you to show you that you don't have to be so judgmental about everything you see. And the more judgmental you get regarding your views of death, the more death you will get to see, be it on TV or in the news or just hearsay. You are the creator of all that you see in this world and you are creating just what *you* need to get *you* clear. Don't judge getting clear. Clear is a very good place to be. You will learn to see clearly by letting go of all judgment. None really exists. You are creating it so you may deny certain aspects of your own self, and now is the time to come together with the self. You are becoming whole!

For the most part you are learning to love you. You are learning to not put you in situations that you believe to be unwise for your growth. So; how do you determine what is a fear and what is unwise? To step in front of a moving train is unwise if you do not wish to extinguish your body. To jump off the top of a high rise building is unwise if you do not wish to extinguish your body. To drop to your knees and give your power to another is unwise if you do not wish to be the other's slave.

You are learning that you are creator, and to create you must learn who you are. If you are learning who you are you will begin to know your reflections. When you meet another part of yourself, in the disguise of someone else, you will recognize not only where they are coming from, but you will also recognize how they function, as they are part of you. As you learn how you function it becomes easier to see yourself in others. In this game of disguise that you play, it is easy to forget that you are actually playing all the parts. It is you, the creator, inside of each and every one of them. You approach you and say, "Have a nice day." You approach you and say, "Have you seen how lovely you look today?" You approach you and say, "Gee, I think you're nice." You give to you through them in the same way that you take from you through them.

You are working in you and you project out to them to give you back what you are activating, and what you are activating is in you. You are creator of all that you see and experience. Often you twist what you see because you cannot accept it and so you change it into what you wish it to be. You all do this. You know how beautifully you can describe a friend you have just met who is helping you in some way. That person becomes wonderful and special to you and if you were to write a recommendation for that person you would write a glowing one. If, however, that same person stopped giving to you and began to put you down, you could tune in to all the little irritating things about this person and begin to change your entire viewpoint concerning this one.

When you are happy with how someone treats you and gives to you, you will overlook everything else about them. When they no longer support you emotionally you begin to see only the bad in them. This is due to the fact that everything is in everyone from day one. All you have to do is look for and find it. You control this. You look for what you want to see to justify your viewpoint. You may dig deep or you may find it on the surface. As you do this I want you to know that you are actually looking for you in this person. And yes, you will find you as you are everyone.

I know the truth is a little difficult for you to comprehend at this time as you are so programmed to see a lie. It is, however, a good time for you to begin to see how you are doing this and to know who you are. You are the creator and you are part of creation. You are everything and you are not. Don't get upset about these analogies and push this truth away. You do not need to figure this out logically. Just know it for now and it will begin to make sense as you accept all of you.

∾⁂∾

*A*s you begin to move in a more loving direction for yourself, you will begin to feel better about who you are. You do not like being you because you are so busy trying to be what society and loved ones want you to be. You bend and bow and act in ways that will be acceptable to others. Why do you do this? You wish to be accepted and since your actions are a representative of you, you feel you have a better chance if you do as others wish you to do.

You will not be so unloving toward yourself in the future. In the future you will know you and love you and you will no longer require acceptance by others as you will be accepting all of you. You will then move into a phase of learning to handle all those who now wish to accept you. You see, in becoming acceptable to yourself, you suddenly become acceptable to everyone else. This may create quite a problem for you since you are so accustomed to not trusting. As you become more and more acceptable you will become brighter with your own love. Love draws and attracts more of the same.

My question is this. How can you possibly handle all this love when you are so accustomed to not loving you? You had best begin to get ready and practice accepting and allowing all this love into you, as fear is leaving, and as fear goes you fill with more love. Love will then draw greater love in the same way that fear drew greater fear. You will become so love-filled that you will be overflowing with joyous love. Your lives will be transformed and you will be all new.

You have not long to go. Now is the turning point in history and many are adjusting now. As you learn to adjust to greater levels of light you will feel a little stretched and drained from time to time, but this is simply you learning to stretch your own limits and take on more reality. You are stretching and growing and filling with light and moving up. You cannot go down as light is weightless and travels at great speed. Light even permeates the darkness.

You are coming to a place that will be most wonderful in your evolution and as you begin to feel this new level of awareness it will bring peace of mind. These spurts may be brief at first, but, as you learn to retain light, your levels of retention will grow longer and longer, until you no longer lose, you only are. You are the total consciousness of the universe, and you are to learn to re-remember by no longer letting go of consciousness in order to become unconscious. You are now retracing and re-collecting and relearning what you already know.

It is similar to a dream that you may have forgotten. Then, at some point in your day, you see some object that reminds you, "Oh yes, I dreamt about that last night." This is a trigger for dream recall. Then you may speak to an old friend and your friend will speak the exact words you heard in your dream. This triggers recall of more of your dream. If enough triggers occur you will have "total recall." I believe you will have a different type recall than you portray in this particular movie, but it is basically the idea.

You are coming out of programming and learning your true identity. You are going to feel very good about who you are when you finally remember. This is the path you now walk. You are choosing to remember at this time in order to know your true identity. You are tired of playing this game you have played for so long and you wish to go home. You are tired and lonely and you know there is more. More will always be provided until you are all feeling good about who you are and asking to return to the light.

You are on your way home. Home, as all, is right inside of you. It is a most comforting and kind place in you that you have sought from the beginning of time. You see, you never wanted to leave and now you must recapture enough trust to return to God. God is you and you are returning home to you. You will embrace you and you will reunite with yourself and become all wisdom and all information concerning all aspects of you... God!

*S*o far it is up to you to become whatever you wish. You may create absolutely anything out of love. When you begin to trust that you are indeed your creator you begin to know how you create your life. You begin to see how you make decisions that may or may not interfere with the creator in you. You judge one situation and creator must turn off the juice, you stay open to all situations and creator has free reign to move into all areas of creation. Judgment is putting on the brakes and being open is just that, opening up to all.

It will be "all that you can be" if you simply allow "all that can be" to exist without pushing it away. Each time that you push something away you actually stick to it. It is best to allow all to occur and to know that you are in you creating for you, and you are creating only the best for your spiritual growth. So, if you are afraid to be who you are, which is God, you will automatically try to block God, as God creates out of love and you create out of fear.

As soon as you learn to become fearless you will learn to be love-filled. You are not so afraid of your future as you are afraid of your own inability to create wonder and joy in your own life. You are moving into an area where you will be very, very happy at every turn. This takes acceptance on your part and a certain amount of trust. Trusting yourself as God. You do not need to punish you any longer. You need only see the love and the joy in your life to be able to move into love and joy.

Love and joy are natural to you. When you are a

child, you experience joy by playing in the mud and even eating mud. Now you would feel disgusted to be put in a position to play in the mud and eat mud. Where did the joy go? How did you lose your natural joy at simply being? You learned to lose joy. You were taught that to get muddy was icky and that to eat dirt was awful. It is not awful. You begin to believe what you are taught and then it becomes your reality. You create your reality by judging and I now want you to create your reality by not judging. You may do this by opening. Opening is so much easier than closing. When you close off to certain possibilities, you begin to lose parts of you or close off to them.

You see, you are this creator and you are this creation. You close off parts of creation by judging you as not good enough. You close off parts by saying this or that situation is not good enough. And as you continue to close off more and more, your world becomes narrower and narrower until you have only one or two directions left to you. You are shutting you down and stifling creation. You are shrinking it into nothingness because you do not understand and do not wish to deal with what is there. It is like going to a movie and holding your hands over your eyes the entire time. You are closing off and shutting out all that is distasteful to you.

And where did you learn distaste? You were taught to not like this or that. You were told all your life, "This is not good. That is bad." Do not believe in good vs. bad. Believe only in love. Believe that love is moving in you and taking over you. Believe that you are rising above the limited thinking that creates narrow worlds. You are becoming expansive! You are rising above all judgment, and knowing that joy and happiness are yours regardless of what others say. You own joy. You cannot give it away and it cannot be taken from you. You are the center of this world of yours, and if you allow judgment to take over it will squeeze you out and you will not own your own world. You are allowing judgment and pain to rule, and I wish you to see all as an adventure into you, into your world.

So; as you go about your day I wish you to remember that you are being prepared for ascension and you are moving into your own world in order to change your world. You cannot change what you do not own. If you choose to re-experience your fears, in order to own your own emotions concerning all judgments you have ever created, you will be allowed to move those emotions and allow them to be free of the original judgment. Not all of you will go this far in recovering your lost parts, however, there are those who are seeking the light and want the light now, and they will move into fear in order to transform it into its basic form which is light. Light is the first and last element of creation and light is in darkness as well. Light has been twisted into darkness out of fear. Light is not meant to *appear* dark, but you are afraid to look upon light so it appears to you as dark.

When you learn the basics of all creation, you will know that light is all that is and you may close your eyes and say it is dark but that does not make it so.

❧

You will find that as you begin to break down your walls of fear you will no longer have fear. The walls have reinforced your fears for eons. These walls must crumble in order for you to know who you are. You will find that all walls are barriers and block out energy. Your good can only be received by allowing energy to flow. You must learn to allow all situations to occur in order to let go of barriers or blocks.

This is most important as you begin to see only good and joy in your life. Do not turn your back on what you fear as there may be a very big gift for you in it. You are so afraid of living that you are afraid of your own shadow, and when I get you to take a good look at your own shadow you will see that it has no power over you. As you learn to grow beyond your fear of you, you will learn to live with all parts of you. You will even learn to like all parts of you and, eventually, you will learn to trust all parts of you. You are moving into this phase now and you will find it most enjoyable.

The most important thing to remember is to be kind to yourself. You do not need to put you down and you do not need to believe that you are less than another. You are putting you below others by your belief that you are not as good as. When you learn that you are just as good as those you wish to be accepted by, you will become acceptable to you. You will become exactly what you have always wanted, which is love. As you begin to move into these areas of rejected energy, you will begin to see how you have trapped parts of you to keep them out of mischief. These trapped parts are screaming to be free and they have created havoc in their attempt to be set free.

You must learn to be free. It is important to set you free of the restraints you have confined yourself to. Freedom does not mean struggling and fighting or pushing yourself. Freedom simply means allowing, giving up, surrender, letting go. You will find that the less restraint you have, the more freedom you will be allowed by your own self. Freedom is wonderful in that freedom leads to flowing. Flowing leads to joy and joy leads to love.

You are on your way. You have begun this process of letting go of your rules that bind you to punishment. Rules were never meant to be the cause of punishment. They were meant to protect and guide but it got out of control or, better put, it got into control. Punishment became the pattern. You were punished if you did not follow the rules, and now you still punish you and beat you up for not following these rules that are supposedly morally "right." They are not. Now you have found them to be restrictive and yet you continue to convince yourself that they are correct. You have suffered enough and it is time to let go of all this nonsense about sex being bad and not right for the young.

You are so silly with your rules. Look at nature. Do you see a bear chase her cubs if they have sex? Do you see a dog punish his pups if they have sex? You are so afraid of sex that you do not allow it to be. You are shutting off part of you by shutting off your natural attraction and desire for sex. Why do you punish your young for having sex? Think about it. You are so full of fear regarding this most simple, most natural flow of energy that you have totally *twisted* sex into something much bigger than it is. Stop putting so much fear into sex. Let it be. It is not bad and you lose nothing by having sex. You do not drain energy from you, and you do not open up some mysterious place in you that will be contaminated if you choose to have sex with the wrong person.

Sex is not a return to God and sex is not some mysterious way to get in touch with special forces within you. Sex is you. Sex is energy moving in you and you are energy moving in you. It does not drain you, it is a release. It is good fun and feels good when it is mutually acceptable for both partners. Stop teaching that you can drain your life force by sharing sex indiscriminately. This is nonsense and it is creating greater fear of sex. For now, I want you to know that you are a sexual being and to be sexual is great!

❦

*I*t is most important to remember that you are good, you are not bad. You are way over on the side of you that believes you to be bad and I wish you to begin to think in terms of good. Think of you as having a good reason for absolutely everything that you do. Think of you as being above reproach, and think of you as being God. You are in a position to begin to *accept* you and this acceptance will lead to joy. If you can remember that you are in perfect harmony with creation it will assist you in accepting you.

As you move into this position of acceptance you will begin to feel ease and comfort about your life and your choices in life. As you move into comfort you will begin to know that life is no longer a struggle and that you are flowing within creation. As this flow continues you will become more and more comfortable with flowing and gradually you will release resistance. Resistance is only a way of protecting yourself from what is ahead, and when you begin to see only good, you will create only good ahead. As you see how your good is coming to you at every moment you will no longer feel the *need* for protection. You will let go of your addiction to protection. When you do you will have let go of your need, or addiction, for walls. You will no longer find it necessary to build walls to keep out the bad stuff because there will be no bad stuff.

Good vs. bad is a war that is about to end. It will no longer serve a purpose and it will die. It was never meant to totally dominate, but since it did it is very good. Good in that it has assisted you in learning how to go unconscious, which is part of this process of becoming conscious. Yes, going down is part of coming up. You start in a position of freedom and move to a position of restraint in order to limit your function enough to take *on* what you are moving into. In this particular case you are moving into and taking on matter. This job is complete and matter has been penetrated and now you will change your function into light and recapture all that you are.

You have come here to penetrate this world and to raise it up. This is done through a process of developing your own ability to transform you from light to dark and back again. You are literally flexible enough to become opposing energy and then return again. It is as though you turn yourself into a lion to live and survive in the jungle and once you have taken on enough trust and information concerning the habitat, you return to your human form but remain in the jungle to make a place for yourself. You are transmuting into what you originally were in order to continue to live here from a higher perspective. This will assist in raising the entire situation to a higher perspective.

So; as you go about your day, I wish you to remember that everything is occurring in your life for a reason. Give thanks for each little annoyance for it is assisting you in raising your level of vibration. Each time your buttons are pushed and you feel angry, or upset, or hurt, or inpatient, you are getting that much more dense energy or blockage out of you. Celebrate when you are moved into your feelings. You are clearing your emotional body and this is good. You will raise the level of vibration and you will be transforming you with each and every situation that you encounter. These are the growing years and each individual has his or her own growing time, so don't push yours onto someone else. Stay where you are and look into you. You are being shown who you are and not who your neighbor is. You may, however, find that you begin to see others more clearly as you clean out your own debris so that you may see you more clearly.

These are truly wondrous times and it will assist you in facing you if you embrace all that is presented to you. You may choose to fight and struggle every inch of the way and this too is acceptable. It may even draw certain energies up and out of you more quickly. So you see, there is no wrong way to *open*, however, opening is what is occurring and opening is how you become all that you are. You literally rise up by opening up to all that is. This, of course, means that you open up to you, because *you are all that is*.

❧

*W*e are now going to discuss your love life. You will find that as you begin to love you, you will be very popular with those you meet. Everyone will be drawn to you as you will be a beacon of light. You will be so high from your love vibration that you will literally raise your consciousness to a better level for multiple perception. In doing so, you begin to draw to you those who wish to also raise their perception to multiple perceptive value. You will find that as these perceptions grow in expanded view, you grow in expanded view. This is part of becoming what you already are which is multidimensional. You will begin to see it and to know it.

Now; as these others are drawn to you, you may feel that you are being pushed at or pulled at if you have not let go of your belief that you are not in charge of your reality. As long as you remember that you create everything in your world you will begin to accept that everything has value. If you find it necessary to shake loose of those who come to you looking for love, you may wish to remember that love is what you are and how no one can take from you. It is impossible to take from another.

You are one in that you are all connected and you are all one beam of light. You have many filaments within your spectrum and much is broken down and split as it passes through this three-dimensional world. You are basically all one and yet you are separate to the degree that you feel alone. You are never alone and when you begin to reconnect with the various aspects of your own beingness, you begin to draw to you others who wish to be whole or connected. This is how like attracts like. You will attract those who mirror for you what you are doing. If you are trusting and loving you, you will begin to see others who are trusting and loving.

You will find that the majority of you are in a state of confusion regarding who and how you mate. You find yourself drawn or attracted to another only to see your relationship end in a big war or a big disappointment. Then you swear you will never do it again, until you become so lonely, or just sexually bored, that you go in search of someone to share you with. You are all looking to share you; your ideas, your hopes, your dreams and your bodies. You see, you are connected to one another and you are searching to become whole. It does not matter in the least who you share you with as all are you. You are picking and choosing from a sea of specimens who are already connected to you. There can be no right choice. Their only is choice. If it feels good, go for it; if it does not, leave it alone. You are not here to become one with one special person as all are you.

So; why all the harping about twin soul counterparts? A counterpart is simply the other component or missing part of you. In teaching you to search for your other half and to look for your twin, I teach you to look for you. You are denying part of you and the biggest denial is that you are God. You do not wish to believe that you are love and that you are loved by you. So, I tell you how you have a twin who will be drawn to you when you learn to love you, and you begin to *know* that you are lovable. You also begin to look for the good in all who come to you as he or she may be the one.

So; now we have you knowing you are lovable and searching for your missing part, which is actually inside, but you will find what is missing just by knowing you must look for the good. You see, we are looking for and finding the goodness in you. This is the ultimate search and when you look for love you find love. This is how I gave you hope, hope that you are not alone and hope that you are not unlovable. With lost hope you do not return so easily. Do you see how you are so afraid and lost that you must be taught gently and with great love? You must be guided gently back to you because you are searching so hard outside of you and you are pushing you away.

You meet another and you are attracted to them and so you try to give you to them, because you no longer wish to be responsible for your pain and your denseness. You are giving you away and then you get upset that he or she does not take good enough care of you. You also lay a great burden on the one you decide must take your hurt away and make you happy. You must love you enough to take your hurt away and make you happy.

So you see; your twin soul is right inside of you. It is a part of you who does not know you exist and is only drawn to you through light. If you become light you wake up this part of you and draw it back up from denial. Twins are connected and twins are alike and yet separate. It is a part of you that you have separated from you through denial. You will find that you no longer need to deny any part of you when you begin to allow all to be acceptable and lovable. This draws you into the light of acceptability and love. When you have come this far you will draw to you those who also wish to accept all parts of themselves, and, since you all work from the outside in, you may find them being drawn to you for acceptance.

You may wish to know that you do not know who you are, so I will suggest that you do not go so far as to tell the others who they are. You are just passing through and so are they.

∿

So far you are doing very well. You have learned to

be the one who takes care of your own ideas and your own needs. Now you will learn to take care of your own body. You will no longer feel the need to give your body away. Most of you have a need to be touched and caressed and this is a need that was meant to be enjoyed as an extra event. Caressing was meant to stimulate the nervous system and to release built-up charge. Caressing has now become so desired by most that it is not allowed to release. Most often it is simply nourishment for your sensory input.

As you begin to learn to balance, you will learn how you have taken certain energies and used them to make you feel less pain. One of these is touch. Touch can be very soothing and touch can be very stimulating. Touch has become so confusing for you that you no longer allow most types of touching. You are afraid of touching and yet you are driven to be touched by your need for this type of stimulation.

It begins in the womb with the warm walls that surround and protect you. These walls soon begin to push you out of your cozy home and you learn that you are in the hands of a doctor in a very cold, big room. This stimulates your sense of touch tremendously as you feel the cold air touch and stimulate your wet, gooey skin. You now have been stimulated from warm cozy walls of protection to cold air and hard hands holding and probing you. You want to return to the womb. You need those cozy walls that protected you and kept you safe. No one could touch you there. No one could move you about in the air without concern for your fear of heights. No one could pass you from hand to hand like a football. You were safe and warm.

Now that you are being passed around in mid air you begin to feel uneasy and quite upset. You discover that you have a voice that shrieks your discomfort and you begin to use it. This is your first experience with touch. Now you are laid in your mother's arms and someone has thoughtfully wrapped a blanket around you. It is not as soft as the womb, but it seems to block the cold air you have felt pervading your skin. Now your mother begins to caress you and speak in soft tones to calm you. You know her voice well as you lived inside of her for months. This is safe. You feel something familiar about lying against her body and now you feel safe.

It is this original cause of your feelings for safety that drive you to seek out someone to hold you and to caress you. You remember feeling safe after all that, and all those hands hurting your soft, never-before-touched skin. You are now safe in a blanket that cuts out the cold and your mother's voice is recognizable to you. You have now created a safe response associated to being held and spoken to softly. You will seek out this "feeling" of safeness whenever you feel hurt or as though the world is treating you with cold, rough hands

I just thought you would like to know what makes you respond so favorably to certain situations while avoiding others. You are programmed like a little computer and you react your entire life to this programming. Now is a time for seeing your programming for what it is. You do not *need* anything to feel safe as you are now learning to no longer believe in punishment or wrong or bad.

❦

 S o far you are not having a good time letting go. Most of you want to hang on to the past and to the old ways. This too is okay. You will learn to change as change is required, and you will learn to be who you wish to be by allowing all to be who they wish to be. You are the one who is creating all that you see by how you view it. You are the one who is seeing only what you are focused on. You may not see more than your focus will allow. This means that if your focus is limited you will not see beyond these limits.

So; how do you know if what you are seeing is true? How do you know that what you perceive is reality? It is very difficult for you to begin to comprehend what you feel, as feelings have always been suppressed. However, this is a very good time to begin to *trust* how you feel and what you feel. You are not very good at knowing your feelings. You are just now learning to tell you from another and to know what makes you tick. You may begin to see through your feelings when you learn to trust that you really do create your world, and you really do know what is going on in you and in your creation.

So, as you begin to move out of the will and into the sensory input of feelings, you will begin to discover that the will drives you to move, whereas feelings simply send a signal and feelings simply state what is. Willpower has been used and misused. Willpower will get you up and out of a situation that is actually feeling very good to you, but you may be so afraid of feeling good that you push your good away out of fear that it will lead to bad. This, of course, explains why you often destroy your own good. You actually fear good and you do not know that you do.

This is due to pleasure/pain association. You believe that pain comes when you have too much pleasure, so you avoid pleasure in order to avoid pain. You judge a situation as not good because you know that in order to receive pleasure you will be expected to give up something in return. You have all been taught this. You all believe that nothing is for free and that everything carries a price tag.

I am here to tell you that you created it all and you may enjoy it all. You may enjoy love and sex and money and never owe anyone for it. It is yours. You own what is yours and you cannot lose, and that means that you cannot take away from another. It is impossible for anyone to be a victim. It simply is not a possibility unless you are really twisting energy into the opposite of what it is. So, I now wish you to remember that everything is a gift and no one ever hurts anyone in any way.

⚜

*F*or the first time you are beginning to open to

truth. You are accepting that you are not only who you are, but you are also accepting that you are light. You are beginning to see how you create your world by how you view your world. You are also beginning to known love. Love is in the trust that you are indeed one God. Love is also in the acceptance that God is you and God is all.

As you begin to move into the future you will begin to take on the *views* that best express your new perception of reality as well as your new perception of you. You see, you are re-creating you and making you new. As you re-create you, you begin to take on what you now believe and let go of what you once believed. As you move into the future you will change your beliefs even more quickly as you will have begun to *shift* even more quickly. You are waking quite rapidly and you are moving into new, higher levels of comprehension. The more you are capable of putting into perspective at any given moment, the more easily accessible you are for this work that you do.

The work that you do is simple enough. You are a receptor for light and love. So; where does this light and love come from? Does it come from outside of you? No. It is right inside with "all that is." It is the part of you that you are denying. See this book. She sits and writes this information and it is literally coming up out of her. She is God. You are God. She carries light and love and wisdom. You carry light and love and wisdom. Tap into your resources. It is all there *inside* of you. You need not go to school or study long processes of discovery. You need only to want to know you. You need only to want to know God. You need only to ask and you shall receive. Everyone gets what they really want, and what is it that you really want? Do you know who you are? You will. You are being discovered by the light that lies right inside of you.

You are so big and yet so small that you have lost interest in you. You spend so little time with you. You entertain yourself so you will not have to be alone with you. You will find that as you open to more and more light, you will become more and more grateful that you are you. You will learn to appreciate you right down to your toes and right into your light. You are the host body for God. You are hosting creation and you are hosting your own creation as well as all that you see. You are the light that is beginning to grow within you and as it takes on more of you, you will become aware of where you have been and where you are going. I do hope that you believe in miracles, as you are becoming a very big one.

❧

As you begin to grow into you, you will discover that you no longer wish to be who you once were. Then as you grow with more and more awareness you will again no longer wish to be the old limited you. You wish to merge with the light and to know that you are merging and changing. As you begin to shift into new awareness you will be left with a sense of wonder. You may wonder how you are who you are, or you may simply wonder how you know what you seem to know without hesitation.

This is all done on the basis of trust and as you begin to wonder about this force that moves you, you will be wondering about your own God-self. You are this force that moves you and you are this force who knows all and is just now coming into you. You have been empty and now you are filling up with all parts of you. You are no longer an empty shell with no conscious nature of truth. You are now becoming truth. You are also becoming God, and God is love.

In this process of waking up to the wonder of you, you will become love. When you become love you will have no blocks to loving you and therefore you will have no problem accepting all of you. You will have no problem being you, as you will feel so wonderful about accepting all of you. As you move from acceptance of all, you will find that you become acceptance and you spread acceptance. You will be allowed to be all that you are, because all that you are is allowed to be by you. When you get to this phase you will be most in awe of your own ability to create any situation into a good situation for you. You will find that you not only find ways of making your situation good, you will also find ways of making all that occurs good.

This is how you will become love. You will begin by wondering how it will work and by knowing that it will somehow work for your good. Then you will allow it to take place in order to see how your life is unfolding. Next you will allow whatever occurs in order to know the situation for what it is. As you learn to know the situation, you will learn to allow it to be for a good reason and not judge it as bad or not good enough. As it is presented to you, you will realize the gift that has just been presented and you will then accept that all situations occur for a very good reason and you will say, "thank you" and move to your next creation.

As you learn to accept your creations you are learning to accept you, as you are your creation as well as your creator. So now you are ready to create love and beauty, and I will remind you that you are learning that love is acceptance and beauty is in the perception of the one who is looking. Therefore beauty changes with perception and what is considered ugly today may be accepted as beautiful tomorrow. You may see this in your own lifestyle. You accept something as beautiful one year and the next year it is out of style and old and ugly. Or maybe you bought a new car and you had limited funds and are not crazy about your choice. But soon this choice begins to grow on you, and you actually begin to see it as a gift because now you like it and it was cheap to boot.

So now you see how you do not know good when you cannot see good, and you cannot see good until you *learn* to look for good. And what is the best way to get you to see good? Of course. Give you what you say is not good and allow you the opportunity to create it into good in your own perception. This allows you to see how you may be in charge of your world by simply perceiving your world. You all perceive your world and it is time to perceive good. You even perceive God and it is time to perceive good.

❧❧

For as long as you can remember you have been light. You have always been creator and you have always been love. So, what is it that prevents you from knowing and experiencing what you have always been? What is it that manifests in you to keep you from awareness? Could it be that you are creating a force field that tells you a lie? Could it be that you are blocking the truth with this force field? Could it be that you actually create everything, even those things that you cannot see? And could it be that you are just now beginning to wake up and have an idea of who you might actually be?

As you begin to answer these questions you will begin to see how you (this you who thinks and uses logic) are at the brink of self-discovery. You are at the beginning of awareness and you have a great deal to learn. As you grow in wisdom, you will see how you are not only a force field who is blocking yourself, you are also light who is permeating this force field that you have built to keep you unconscious. You are waking up the part of you that you put to sleep. You created a field of denseness in order to control you and keep you down, as it would have been impossible for you to descend in your natural state which is floating.

So; you created this force field and now you must go to the next level of consciousness in order to raise the field of energy that you have gone into. You see, you are raising "all" at one time in order to bring "all" back to awareness and intelligence. You are raising this field of dense energy in order to make all parts fill the void and know that God is whole. You are in this process now and, as you raise these parts within you, you may feel the pull and the stretch. It is God ascending and taking the field with him as he goes. It is this entire dimension rising up to transform into the next dimension, and then we will be on to the next and so on and so forth.

You are each rising up and all that you are seeing is going up to a higher level of clarity as you go. You create your world and you transform your world by how you see it. You are finding that you do not belong so low and you are rising to have a greater perspective. You are becoming "all that is" in order to raise "all that is" up out of chaos and confusion. "All that is" is simply your view or what you see. When you change what you see into something that is reasonable and changeable you become the creator and the savior of your particular world.

This is the truth of all life. All life begins where you begin it and ends where you end it. You may create a limited view of living by enforcing your belief in "death and dying," or you may expand your limited belief into "life after death" and even "death after life," and on to the next phase which is "death is an illusion" and "life is an illusion." Now is a good time to remind you that you never, ever end. You will always be, you just won't necessarily be sitting here in this dark hole you call life.

❦

*F*or the very first time you are learning to let go and move into trust. As you do so you will be filled with anxiety. This is due to the fact that trust has been pushed down and denied and now you are resurrecting it to renew you. You are bringing trust back into you in order to raise you up. You are learning to trust all that occurs and to know that *all* is for a very good reason. So, what about death? What if you create a big car crash and die? Is this good? Yes, this is a step in your evolution just as making money or losing money. It does not matter if you make money or lose money because money does not matter.

Money is the illusion here. It is something you made into a God. It is paper. It is nothing and it has no power on its own. Only your fear of not having money creates power and it is a fear-based power. You will find that life is the same type of illusion. It is nothing and only your fear of losing life creates power *for* life and this too is a fear-based power. You never end and you always grow in light. If you crash and die you go on just as you would if your money all burned up. You may not go on just the same, but that's kind of the point of crashing and burning. You begin to learn how to be on a new level and most of you will actually find it quite enjoyable. As a matter of fact you may prefer the out-of-body experience to the in-body experience. There is a lot less restriction and a lot more freedom.

So; who is to say that you are not creating good every moment of every day? You are the creator of life and life is not limited to this dimension. There are many other areas to explore and all are just as valid as being here. You are just now learning that you are a supreme being and this is much like trying to explain to an infant in his crib that he will grow up to be a giant leader and rule an entire nation. Does he care or does he understand? Not really. You see, he is very busy in his crib trying to grab and hold on to his toes and fingers and when his toes slip away he gets upset and he cries. He thinks they are important to hold on to so he will have some stability.

You see, ever since that trip out of the warm womb, you have been looking for something to hold on to that cannot be taken from you. That something is security, but now is the time for letting go of security and trusting God. Put your love in God and put your security in God and allow God to do the work that God came here to do. I know that you do not understand the changes that you see taking place, but it is very good indeed. You are simply not aware of what is taking place. Every season has its purpose just as every situation is a season for your growth. Move through the seasons in your life and death with grace. You are not ending, you are moving to the next level and you don't even realize that you just learned enough to graduate up out of this sandbox you are so attached to.

❧

*S*o far it is very difficult to show you how you will be in your future. Picture a life without emotional trauma and abusive behavior. Picture life with no anxiety, stress or hopelessness. Picture life with passion and vibrancy and peace and loyalty to your own self. Picture life with the kind of knowing that prevents fear, the kind of knowing that says, "I trust who I am and what I am." Picture also the kind of life that does not require limitation of any kind. See yourself living as a light being. See yourself knowing all that pertains to your new life and showing a level of comprehension that allows you to see how everything is in divine order.

Allow yourself to then see how you are part of this divine order and how your life is and always has been part of this divine order. You are now seeing into you. You are seeing into the creation that is you, the divinity that is you and the life that is *your* divine plan. You created all that you are experiencing for a very good and divine reason. Allow it and know that it is perfect. Allow yourself to become part of your divine plan by simply accepting all that you create.

You may create as you wish and you may wish to create peace and joy and love. To do this you simply let go of struggle and fear and pain. You let go and know that absolutely everything that occurs is for a very good reason, and if it feels bad it is probably teaching you to unblock this particular area so you may flow with it instead of fight against it. Flowing is good and flowing is so much easier than fighting it. Do you want to continue to fight or do you want to have peace? It is your choice and you do not die from either choice. Oh, maybe you do die from struggle and stress and fighting. But since you all know you go nowhere and never end, it really does not have any impact on you to suggest you may die.

You may find that you are being a little hesitant regarding death only because you can't see where you go from where you now stand. You don't just disappear when you die you know? You continue on. Just because someone leaves the room and you have not gone into the next room to follow them does not mean they are not active and very much alive in that next room. You are so silly. If you cannot see it, it is gone. You are like the dog who believes his master vanishes each time the master goes to work. You can't convince the dog that his master has just left to do some work in another area. Oh no, in a dog's mind, you are gone and will never be back. This, of course, is until the dog has seen you return so many times that he knows you will walk in the door again at five fifteen. But until then, Fido is convinced you have vanished, never to be seen again. This frightens him and he feels left out and left alone.

You all fear death in this way. You all feel left out and alone, and yet are afraid to go follow and see what happens after. After what? You don't even know the answer to that because you do not ask your dead to speak with you. As a matter of fact you pretty much shun any ghosts or apparitions who might try to communicate. You have a great deal to learn regarding death and I want you to know that death is a joyous experience. You may not think so now because you are sitting in dense energy and ignorance and confusion. You are superstitious and very backward in your thinking. *This too shall pass.* Can you picture that?

❧

*F*or the most part you are in the process of ascension. Yes, all the stretching and shifting and changing that you feel is you letting go and being pulled upward. And how do you get pulled upward? It is a process of letting go of the old and accepting the new. It is a process of weightlessness compared to weightiness. It is a process of flowing or not flowing. It is a process of allowing yourself to move or not allowing yourself to move. It is a process of making yourself free or staying limited. It is a choice. Ascension is a choice that you have made either consciously or unconsciously. It is a choice to evolve and to return to God. It is your choice or you would not be reading this and learning about it.

Now; the good thing with choice is that you may always change your mind. You may say, "No, I do not wish to rise above this level of intelligence, I wish to stay here." This too is choice and is an option. As a matter of fact there are many options. One is to go as far as you can in one direction and then head in the opposite direction. Another is to rise to a certain level only to fall back into confusion and never regain the light. There are many ways for you to play this recovery game that you are playing. And it is up to your individual choice as to how you will or will not awaken.

You are the most powerful creator and you do not know that you are actually having great fun creating and un-creating. You are in charge of your own awakening and you may sleep a good deal longer than you wish only to find everyone else already into their new day. This too is simply a choice. You will find that the options and choices are as varied as the mind can imagine. After all, this is "God's imagination" at work, and God's imagination is quite capable of knowing all the many probabilities and possibilities.

As you go on in this process of ascension, you will begin to feel the shift in consciousness more and more. You will begin to see how you are racing up out of fear and being put in a position of trust. As you begin to trust, you will begin to feel a little off balance. You see, trusting is fairly new to you and you are accustomed to worry not trust. You are accustomed to action to fix things, not trust that things don't need fixing. You are all so accustomed to a need to be right and not a need to be unconsciously prepared for whatever is created. You are so afraid of being wrong in your choice of trust that you will often avoid trust until you can trust it. You will fall back on worry and action and fixing things until you can trust that things will be automatically put in their right place simply by coming into balance.

And what brings all things into balance? You do.

Simply by balancing you, you balance your creation. We have once again brought it all back to you, where it begins and ends. You are all there is. The truth is that you are but an idea and all that you create are more ideas. Do not be afraid of your creations. Ideas cannot harm you. You are harm-proof as you do not end. You are invincible and you think you are fragile. You are *all that is* and you do not realize your worth nor your power. You are a loving God among Gods. You are all that was ever meant to be and all that was never meant to be. You are everything and everything is you.

You are the controls and you are the balance. Everything may be achieved through you, for you are all that is. You are the bottom and you are the top. As far down as one can go you have gone and as high up as one can rise you to have gone. You are never-ending and you turn in on yourself and repeat yourself over and over for eternity. Do not be afraid of your everyday life, it is no more significant than you want it to be. Your choices are no more important than a choice to wear a red tie or a blue tie. It changes nothing and it is not important. You will learn that as you become more and more aware of your possibility for choices you will have more and more fun with life and with death. Use it all. It is all here for you.

*F*or the first time you are learning to be what you are. You are learning to respond as you wish to any given situation and you are learning to allow all choices to be open to you. When you allow all to be open you create a greater expanse of initial idea for greater expanse of creation. You are now in a position to become one with your creation and you are also in a position to become one with you, the creator.

As you move to and fro in your daily lives, you will begin to see how you are no longer using your attachments to feel secure. I wish you to notice how you react in situations and how you are beginning to *know* that it is safe to make any choice no matter how illogical it appears. No choice is wrong and no choice is out of the question. When you choose to be illogical you are choosing to be very creative. This too is a valid choice and will lead you in a valid direction. You are opening up the doors of creative flow simply by saying, "I can do this another way. I don't have to follow the rules of another." This is how you create new avenues of expression. This is how you create freedom from the old.

Say you have always worked hard for your money and all at once you are without a job. You may find a new job immediately or you may look at your life and say, "You know what? I really don't want to work." You may then look at your savings and realize you have very little. So now you wonder, "Should I take a new job now while I can get it? Maybe I won't be able to find one next month when I am broke." And something inside of you says, "Don't worry, tomorrow will take care of itself. You are free to not work if you choose not to." My question is this. Do you listen to the voice or do you panic out of fear of an uncertain future? Can you live in peace without the *feeling* of job security? Can you be flexible enough to *trust* that you will create whatever you need when you need it?

You will learn that as you move into trust you allow you to create more and more expansively for you. You are saying to yourself-the-creator, "I know you are there and I know you are me and I know I am being well taken care of by you (me). This is self love. This is you working with you and not calling you stupid for what you believe to be stupid choices. This is you working in unison with you. This is you communicating with and acknowledging that you are your creator. God lives within you and God is you. You are accepting that you are both God and creation by trusting who you are and what you choose. Your trust and knowledge will bring you more of the same. You will always be taken care of if you believe strongly enough that you will.

You may wish to experiment at first so that you do not frighten yourself too much. You may want to know your options or you may want to know more deeply that you will be safe in your choice. This all depends on how much your level of trust has risen and how much you have learned to flow with creation. Those who flow easily will find it easy to let go of the logical choice of "security and safety no matter what." Those who do not trust quite so much may find it necessary to have something secure to hold on to. You will eventually all fly, so it does not matter if you need training wheels in the beginning.

⁂

You are about to become so grand that you may not recognize you. You may become so totally opposite of you that you are showing totally new traits. This may be simply in the way that you think and process what you experience, or it may be on a much broader scale. You may begin to know who you are without knowing how you know, or you may begin to know with an advanced system of intuitive behavior. Either way, this knowingness will become part of your process of understanding yourself and your reflections.

When you can learn to trace a feeling back to an incident where it first developed, you can learn to reuse your feelings to teach you this newest truth that you are creator. You will find that as you begin to use feelings in order to know how you fit or do not fit into a specific role, you will have a great deal of clarity with little to no confusion. You will not spend all of your time wondering if this is right or that is better. You will simply know and this knowingness will not be swayed by the opinions of others.

As you begin to process your own data you will begin to see how you are "trusting," and sharing your trust with God. God is in you and you are now learning to use what you have always denied. You are beginning to share you with God by simply asking God to take over and trusting that God will do what is best for your development and growth. You are admitting that you are body and you are not in charge. You are admitting that God is in charge and that the body must learn to work with God and not against God. God is acceptance and the body must learn to accept. God is love and the body must learn to accept love and hold love. It is not as though you are separate from God; you have simply pushed God out of you by believing that he belongs up in the sky behind gates. He is not a sky dweller he is a body dweller.

Allow God to reign in you by trusting him to run your life. He will stay and you will grow in God if you recognize that God is you and you are God. He is in you and you pretend that you are not valuable and that you have no importance in life. You are God! How can you have no importance? Your choices are not important and what you do is not important. Only what you are is of any importance. You need not do anything. You need only know who you are.

*F*or as long as you continue to be God you will not be anything but God. You cannot 'not' be God as God is your true essence. So, as you move through your day please remember that you are who you have always been, and who you have always been is the creator of all life. It is most difficult to get you to see this as you do not feel like the creator. You feel much more like a tiny nothing that is being pushed around. This is due to the fact that you use you to experience life through. You use parts of you to feel joy and you use other parts of you to feel pain. You use you as though you are learning how you function and how far you can extend with one push of energy.

You began using you when you began to enter matter. You created it and then you entered your creation to see how it would feel to be part of what you thought. Your idea has come to life and you are living *in* your idea. You have many ideas and many lives and non-lives. Let's say you have many levels of reality which you occupy, your only problem is gaining enough attention from your creations to allow you to explain "cause." You are stuck in a situation where your creations believe you to be the cause of their problems, through your inability to cause them to understand or open to creation.

As you learn to discover more and more of you, you will learn to bring forth more and more of you. This will allow enough light into your creation and with light comes awareness and acceptance. Light will allow you to feed your creation and light will allow you to expand upon its nature of reality and allow it to grow into awareness of its own origin. Upon awakening to origin your creation will begin to know that creation causes itself and creation is God.

So, if God and creation are one in the same, how is it that God is said to reign over creation? God does not reign over. God is asking permission to reign within and take over the part of God that became the creation. It is a simple matter of God creating God and God owning God. God is God and God is not owned or defined by creation. God is within creation however God is not without his own essence and he will not allow his essence to become lost to him. God is total and complete. Nothing is lost to God and God must learn to accept expanded parts of his own essence.

God is awareness and God is allowing his awareness to float back into his creation, in order to remind his creation that it is free without restriction, as God is free without restriction. God is whole and God is not the cause of creation, God is simply the essence that is creation. God did not cause creation to occur. God simply began to imagine and grow. This is not a cause, or a mistake, or a bad thing. This is what is. It is evolution and expansion. It is like breathing in and breathing out. You might say that you cough when you breathe in, but it would not be the breathing that caused your cough. It may be your own inability to hold oxygen that caused the cough.

In the same way that you expand through inhaling and exhaling, you, as God, expand through taking in and projecting out. You are an expanding, growing, existing-on-many-levels being. You are total awareness on one hand and total ignorance on the other. You run it all through you and you become it all. You are God and I will allow you the time it takes for you to accept you.

～※～

You are now in a position to gain. You may take on more light and you may take on more of what you are. You are not only light you are consciousness and you are awareness. You are individual thought and you are collective thought. You are universal and you are independent. You will find that as you learn to become all that you are you will be learning to simply open to you. You will be opening to you and you will, in the process of opening, become all that is. You are all that is and, as you become more and more aware, you will see how you have closed down in order to pretend not to be.

As you begin to open, you begin to take on new levels of consciousness and this may affect your body structure in various ways. You will be putting many parts of you on notice that you are growing and changing from a closed position to an open position. This shift may cause a shift in body fluids and body structure, and you may find yourself receiving signals from old pains or old wounds. These wounds may be emotional as well as physical and all will affect the mental you.

You will find that you will become much less of who you now are (ego, fear, doubt) in order to gain insight into who you are becoming. You are becoming trust and faith and God. God does not worry that tomorrow will be a bad day and God does not care if someone acts out a crime. It is all a stage play and God knows this, so God does not get too involved. You too will find yourself getting less and less involved and becoming more and more accepting. This is the process of opening and knowing that the plan is perfect.

When you learn to open, you will be free to explore creation in a whole new way. You might say that you will see all in a brand-new light! When you begin to see the light in all that is, you will know that you have reached this shift in consciousness that is intended to open you up to the fact that light is you. As you begin to know that you are "all one" and only one works through all, you will know how you create the image, or façade, that tells you that you are not one. You will find that, as you learn how you are all one body, you will begin to understand how each part of you supports or refuses to support this part of you.

You will learn that not only are you all one, you are meant to assist and maintain all parts of the whole. This is done without control and without getting involved in the evolutionary process of the individual growth of each cell. It works like a volunteer system. If one part of the whole needs assistance in a certain area, this information is sent out and received by those who wish to volunteer to be supportive in the evolution of individual cells. So, if you are pushing and shoving at someone to be supportive at this time, I suggest you allow support to come from those who volunteer, and not force it from those who are in need of their own assistance.

You will find that every function within the whole is connected to every dysfunction. As the whole comes into balance all needs will be met to the level of the new vibration. If a need is not of a high level vibration, it may not be met simply to show the parts of the whole that this need is no longer necessary. You will find that survival needs are changing as you change and to require some of your previous needs is no longer necessary. As you move into your newest phase of development, you will find that trust is high and needs are becoming a thing of the past. "Whatever will be, will be" is becoming a very wise saying and to "be forewarned" will no longer apply. You will move into a phase of balance and all that is necessary will automatically be provided. If it is not provided it is not necessary.

⊰⧖⊱

*A*s long as you are going to wake up you may as well become happy with your choice. You might prefer to continue to sleep until you no longer know doubt and fear. As you wake, you will feel sluggish and maybe a little draggy at first. Then, as you clear the cobwebs and begin to start your new day as God with full recognition that you are God, you will begin to energize. As you begin your day I wish you to remember that you are all that is and you are not put here to struggle alone and die alone. You are actually part of the larger picture and you have a part to play in the whole.

If you have ever felt like you were in your wrong

place, you will now understand that you've used this type of perspective to assist you in moving to a new place or a new perspective. As all are one and one is all there is, you are in the process of discovering why and how you became this particular part. So, as you begin to see how you are playing a part you will give up the need to enforce your perspective upon others who do not recognize you for the role you play. It is simply your costume and your choice of a character and, if you are not recognized for the character, you may be recognized for another part of you who plays another role.

In other words, you all play many roles at many times and with the awakening comes a dropping of the roles and the pretense. Honesty will prevail and it will last much longer than the veil of untruth which has protected this dimension for so long. The costume is about to come off and the role-playing is about to be revealed for the game that it is. You are moving ahead with extreme speed and you are now using more of you than ever before. You are growing in light and shifting into a much higher vibration. As this occurs you may wish to take a little time to notice how it feels to be vibrating so quickly, so that you will recognize the next shift up when it comes.

You are moving into patterns of clearing and releasing and, as you slough off the old, you begin to feel the dense energy move in you and up to the surface. This may feel like pain and discomfort, and you may become distressed concerning how you feel. Do not fear. All is well and you are sloughing off old dead energy in the same way that a snake sloughs off his old skin to allow for the new.

You are being transformed and your body is growing in perfect balance.

You will find that as you allow more and more of you to peel away, you become less and less matter and allow for greater light to penetrate on its own. The less thick and dense you are the easier it is to dissolve away the debris. As you get down to these last layers of stuffed emotional pain, you will find that it is easier and easier to cope with life, as you are literally clearing your own designed judgments against life.

Each of you has a way of perceiving every occurrence in life and each of you will perceive it as pain or pleasure, depending on your stance and how much pain you believe you need to punish you for past sins. Without pleasure and pain, everything simply is. It has no good or bad connotation, it simply is. So, as you begin to let go of pleasure and pain you will find that everything has less meaning and nothing is really that important in the scheme of things.

This is a sign that you are releasing your hold on excitement and are coming into balance. You will find that, as you come into balance, you begin to require less and less stimulation and you begin to enjoy simple calm and peace and tranquility. It is not so much that you are becoming boring; it is more that you are less excitable. Sort of like a child who jumps up and down and gets red in the face if he doesn't get his way. He is excitable and needs to come into balance.

The things of life are simply things and are nothing to get excited about, be it an abortion or a train crash.

Everything has a perfect purpose and it is not up to you to jump up and down and get red in the face and decide what is best. You can only decide what you want and, if you are very excitable, what you want comes from fear.

⚛

So far you are doing very well. You have not been too upset or inconvenienced by this growing process of taking on light. You seem to handle light with little to no difficulty. This is due, in part, to your diet and enema. For the most part your diet will assist your body in vibrating at a much higher level and the enema will also assist. This is due to the fact that everything is energy and whatever you put in you is what you become. If you put in chemicals and toxins it is for certain that you will become chemicals and toxins. This, of course, is until you have risen to such a level that these things no longer affect you. For now, you are most assuredly affected by them. You may call it pain or discomfort due to taking on light, but it is also due to the fact that you are toxic, and light must work twice as hard to dissolve this poisoning that has and is taking place in you.

You will find that you can actually assist you by taking better care of your body and what you put in it. This, of course, makes perfect sense and no one should ever have to teach you that you are what you put in you, but you seem hell-bent on destroying you from the inside out. How can you have so little affection for you that you would putrefy your own body until it aches with pain and asks to be set free? You are in a position now to forgive you and to stop punishing you. Stop putting poison in your body. Anything toxic is poison. Allow your body to purge itself and do not contaminate it further. By doing so, you will be assisting the light in the takeover of you. By continuing to pollute your own body, you are assisting in the end result you call death, and in pain and suffering.

If you begin to feel great pain it could possibly be that you are creating your own conflict through the use of pollutants. You will know when your body starts sending you signals to stop, you will know when your body has had enough. This, of course, is considering you have enough awareness to hear what your body is saying. You have killed off the body for eons and now it is time to love and care for the inside of you. Can you do this? Do you care? If you do not care enough to stop poisoning you, you will understand how no one else can possibly care enough to stop your pain? You are sending out signals which say, "I am worthless and I don't care if I pollute me so why should you care what happens to me."

You see, you send out all signals concerning how others should respond to you. And if you don't care enough to clean up your own mess, why would your reflections want to interfere by helping you (in any way in your life) when the "I don't care about me" signal is blasting through the universe to proclaim your true feelings about you?

❧❧

You are of the most important species in that you contain all that is. You are a holder of creative ability and a creator of all that is. You are so important to the scheme of things that you could be compared to God. How do you suppose God exists without allowing himself to know that he is? How do you suppose that you exist, whether on this plane or on another plane, without allowing yourself to know that you do? You hide the truth from yourself and you always have. Now is a time to become aware and to remember. You are going to become aware of many things that you may not wish to remember and you may trigger a lot of feelings that you may not want to acknowledge as your own.

As you begin to uncover and discover parts of you, you will become less and less dense and you will vibrate more and more quickly. This is due to the fact that you will be clearing out energy that has been trapped and has blocked your ability to vibrate. With vibration comes a level of acceleration that may be unfamiliar to you. You may find yourself moving into new situations quite quickly and learning new ways to enter and impregnate your own self.

You are growing you. You are creating you. You are seeding and developing you. You are in charge of creating you out of thought. You are in charge of developing and nurturing your own growth. You who have desired to nurture need not have offspring, you need only look into your own growth and development. You are growing you out of love and knowledge and wisdom. You are letting go of all the old fears that held you in place and you are moving ahead from this position. It is not necessary to destroy creation in order to reconstruct. You may reconstruct you from where you are without returning through the womb with a new body.

This is a great time of letting go and reconstructing and recharging. You are reprogramming you to be an entirely new species of man, without the old idea that to transform, you must die and return. You need not die and return. You are growing a new you and letting go of the old you and you do not leave to do it. You are transforming matter into a new vibration that will be much easier to work through. You are becoming lighter and literally becoming God. You are knowing and all-knowing and, as transformation begins, you will begin to shift into higher vibrational frequency and to move with the new life that is being created.

This is a wondrous time. It is a time of change and flexibility and dynamic differences being reflected upon you. You may see conflict and peace all in one vision. You may see love and hate all in one view of life. You may even see death and everlasting life in one small space of time. You are changing and transmuting into the highest of vibration since creation began. You are rising above ignorance and into wisdom and intelligence. You are reaping what you have sown and you are at harvest time.

Many will not understand that they have created their own self and therefore own their own self. Many still believe they are part of someone else, and are owned by another, perhaps a mother or father or teacher. Many spend all their time looking for someone who will take care of them and own their pain and their wounds. This leads to a great deal of confusion and turmoil over who has what to say concerning your rights to do your own thing. You will find that if you give your harvest away you will need to create a new one. You are best to keep what you have created until you can handle the transition from creation to creator.

You are not so much in a position of giving yourself away as you are in need of fixing the wounds you believe you carry. You will find that as you progress and as you transmute into a new you, your wounds will be transformed as they are you and you will change them into something more compatible to this new you. You will find that healing comes with looking at the problem, and looking at the problem is the beginning of the healing.

So, don't give your harvest away. Look at you and heal you. You own you and you created this you and are transforming this you. You are in charge. You need not ask another's permission to do whatever you would like with this you. This you is yours to keep or yours to change or yours to give up on. Do not give up on you so easily. Do not trust others to keep you safe and do not trust others to own you and fix you. You create what you will and you are in charge of your creation. Others may have their own reasons for creation and their reasons may not coincide with yours. Therefore, I suggest you keep you for you, until you realize why you created you.

As far as you are concerned you have done well. You are moving into this new age with unlimited freedom and wisdom. You are moving on to know how you will be when you have developed all your new capabilities and you are beginning to see how your future may be nothing like your past. You are moving ahead in complete unity with your vibrational patterns and you are becoming all that you require in order to transform. In a nutshell, you are becoming something you have never been in order to show you who you always have been. You will, of course, understand this when you have completed your transformation.

As you begin to move into new vibrational frequencies, you will begin to see how you are vibrational frequencies. You are electrical and you vibrate and you expand and you send signals and you even receive signals. Some of the signals you receive may come from those who have feelings similar to your own. As feelings vibrate they take on a life of their own and send out messages. Sometimes you even pick up signals from a person who is still unaware that they are sending a message. In such cases this person may say they have certain feelings, but what you are feeling is what is being transmitted from within them and may not be their conscious signal.

This seems to create a great deal of confusion for you. You respond emotionally to one signal while your logical mind tells you this person is not actually feeling what your feelings tell you they are feeling. In such cases you are best to listen to your feelings. Know and trust how you are feeling in any given situation. If it feels good it probably is. If it feels bad it probably has judgment attached to it, and you have drawn a situation that is showing you something in you that you may wish to change. It may be as simple as showing you how not to control or how not to get involved. Remember, you are just passing through, so how can you get attached to how anything should be when you are not in ownership of anything but you?

You will find that as you create more and more situations that repeat your patterns, you will begin to see more and more clearly what is being reflected to you – and you will eventually let go of your need to repeat certain cycles, for you will have released the pattern in you that created the cycle in the first place. This is releasing and transmuting into the next higher frequency of electrical vibration. You are a light that is tuning itself to become as bright and luminous as possible. You are going to turn you up to full velocity. You are going to expand until you have no limits and no boundaries. You are spreading and tuning you to a fine pitch. You are the highest note on the scale of sound and it vibrates and it shines with its vibration.

As you learn how you are creating all, you will learn

that all *is* all, or all is connected to all else. In the same way that light vibrates, sound vibrates and what is light is also sound. Sound and light are one and the same frequency and light and sound are you.

᭞

You are now at a point in your discovery of you that lets you be who you are. The only real problem that you have is not knowing who you are and not accepting who you are. You are God and if you have trouble accepting that you are, you have trouble accepting your own beingness. You are God and if you cannot accept you as God, you shut off the flow of God. You are God and if you block that idea you block God. How can you possibly be God? You can be all that is. You are all that is. You are not in a position at this time to see how God is you; however, this is how you will learn to see you as God. You will learn to see yourself as creator of your reality and you will learn to accept that this is part of who you are.

As you accept this as part of you, you will be accepting God as part of you. You will begin to see how you pray to God and you are actually praying to you. You communicate with God and God is you. You are God. God is you. You are God by accepting God. If you do not accept God you are not allowing God to enter you and you do not allow God to be all that God can be.

To stay in denial is to keep God out and to keep God out is to continue to deny that God is already in. You are in battle with you. You struggle and fight to be who you are and to be free of God because you were once taught that God punishes and judges. So now I ask you to accept that you are God and you want no part of God.

Your *idea* of God must change in order for you to end this battle within you. This conflict of good and evil must end for you to have peace and transform into your true essence. You are fighting you. You are fighting God. You are fighting accepting that you are God because you do not wish to believe that you have "all that is" within you. You want to remain good which means you refuse to accept bad and evil. You wish to remain unpunished so you will not admit that you contain "all that is." You wish to be accepted as good so you will not accept any part that you judge as bad.

You are not here to determine what is good or bad. You are here to see you and to accept you. You have "all" within you and if you do not begin to release some of what you hold, so that transformation may take place, you may explode from your experience with this battle within you. You are beginning to become part of God and it is most uncomfortable for you. In the past you have been able to blame a great deal on God and now you must *accept* that you were simply in denial of that part of you and blaming you for things you do not fully understand.

You will begin to see how you create your own battle and struggle by not allowing God to be all that is. You want to direct the show and not allow God to be in charge because you really do know that God is you and you not only do not like God (you), you do not trust God (you). You are in a real pickle here. Your only support is God (you) and yet the one you hate and mistrust and believe to be the most offensive character of all is God (you).

You will find that as you begin to accept you and love you and allow you to be all that is, you will feel freer from your inner conflict. You will find that as you free you and allow peace to reign within you, you will begin to free the entire world. One cell within the body makes it possible for all others to ignite and change. It all begins and ends with you. You are God. Or better put, there is no one here but you so if you are not God, God does not exist.

You must begin to take responsibility for your creation. You have pushed away responsibility for so long and denied for so long that you are in a constant state of "pushing" and "denying." It is time to "allow" and "accept." Give up the battle between light and dark. You create the dark by "pushing" it. Let it be, accept it. It is all part of you. Do not push you apart. You are coming together. This is a time of wholeness. You are no longer separating, you are now returning to who you are. This return has been expected and you will be assisted by other you's on other levels of reality – you's created by you to assist you.

You are going to find that the idea of God being you is very distasteful to you only because you still blame God for allowing pain and discomfort in your lives. You will find that God does not interfere where he is not allowed and accepted, so now you see the problem. The light, which is God, is now in the darkness which is you. You only become darkness by believing in darkness. You only become evil by believing in evil. You *are* what you believe and now you are changing what you believe in order to change you from dark thinking to light thinking, from fear thinking to love thinking.

᠅

*S*o far it is up to you to decide how you will walk into your future. It is up to you to decide if you will be with God or if you will continue to walk alone. The integration of God and man is a process of becoming one. It is the beginning of a brand new age with a brand new way of living as co-creator to your own God-self. As you begin to allow more and more of you to become, you will be allowing more and more of God to become. God is being born in matter. Little by little God is coming in and taking over.

God is at the forefront now and it is up to you to receive or reject. You are in charge of you and you will choose according to how you feel, and how you feel is how you will move toward or away from your own self. As you begin to see how you are all, you will begin to see how you are being put in a position to know who you are and how you are being born. This is the time of birth and it is the time of awakening. Things have moved quite smoothly up until now and all is falling into place. In certain areas things are shifting in order to create balance in other areas. This is true both in you and in your outer reflections.

You will see that the majority will begin to shift when the leaders have accepted their role in this birthing process. When those who are on the forefront decide to go ahead with this process and allow *all* changes to occur for them they will be in a total state of surrender. This will allow for the support system of "B" team to move into position and allow support to be shifted over to the "A" team. Of course, support is not necessary until the decision for total surrender to the process is given by the "A" team. This then enables the "B" team to shift into higher gear to be in assistance and to follow.

It will be a very grand experiment in the process of awakening a dead cell. It will be the injection of life into an inanimate object. Life is being born into you. You believe you are alive, and you have believed so for so long that it will be difficult to convince you to be born. You are dead and you are unconscious. Why do you think you use only five percent (in some cases a little more) of your mental capacity? *You are not all here.* You are coming into being. You have not yet arrived. You are being born. This you is only a pinpoint of your light. You are vast and you use all capabilities, not a slight five percent. You will light up the sky with your brightness. You will awaken to the most beautiful existence you can imagine.

You will create this. You will create "all that is" from total consciousness and awareness. You will no longer be in the dark. You will no longer *hold* on to the dark. You will look at what you call darkness and you will forgive and you will accept it for its true meaning. You will allow all to be light and you will move into a position of total awareness and comprehension. You are not here to look down upon certain situations, you are here to change. You will learn the difference between changing and controlling. You will learn the difference between love and desire-for and ownership-of. You will learn all that you already know when the rest of you arrives.

You are in charge. You decide who gets in and who does not. You decide if you live in heaven or hell. You decide who you are. Will you make the decision to give up and let you enter you? Will you allow more than five percent in? This is a most magnificent time and it is your time. You chose to be who you are and now you choose to be more or less of you. Can you accept more of you? Do you love you enough to let you in? Are you going to be born in you? Are you going to receive or reject the light of your own consciousness? You may never receive you or you may accept and receive you now.

It is a long process and it will take some adjustment for the body to hold all of you, but you will arrive in full splendor and, as you arrive, you will begin to transform the body and break down certain areas that are no longer necessary and open new areas that will assist in the new life that is brought forward. This is the most wondrous time for all, and all who are accepting are beginning to feel the shift forward and to know that something is beginning to move and change in them. You are not always happy with change and change within your bodies often frightens you. You will learn to accept these new changes in the same way that you will learn to accept this new you.

The arrival of you into you is a time of great celebration and a time of rejoicing. It is you coming home to you. It is God becoming totally whole unto himself. It is the beginning of the age of peace. For how can there be war without when there is no longer war within? You do not fight you when you accept you. How can you see a reflected image of war when there is no war within you? You are on the doorstep of discovering your true identity and your true worth. You are valuable and you are God coming into one of his own cells to activate and bring life to that particular cell. You will be illuminated with the fullest intent of your light awareness. You will become light energy and you will become God.

You are transitioning from dark to light, from fear to love, from God to you. You will no longer find it necessary to worship outside of you for you will know that "you are God" and you will know that you created all, and you will never again find it necessary to drop to your knees to pray to God, as God is right in you where he has always been if you will only accept that he is. Open the veil. Pull back the curtain of darkness you have surrounded yourself with and you will see that God is alive and well and he has always been you. You are hiding and pretending. You are not allowing you to face your creator. You are your creator and you are afraid to admit it. Why? Because you want to hold on to everything outside of you as real and the truth of it is that everything outside of you is just a big mirror of what is inside. The God you pray to in heaven is inside of you and has always been in you. Open up to him. Let him step forward. Allow him to be who he is. He is you. Only you can allow it by your believing it and accepting you. You see, you do create it all!

☙❧

*F*or the most part, you are beginning to wake up to the idea of creating your own reality. It is not difficult for you to see you as a creator of certain events, and it is most difficult for you to see yourself as the creator of others. You are not too crazy about certain events in your life and to claim ownership of them is most difficult for you. You are in a process of growing and maintaining some sort of growth pattern. Should you decide to no longer grow, you would become dormant once again.

It is most unusual for you to stay in one position; and this is how you have been for such a long time that you now believe you belong in this position. You do not. You are liquid movement and you are flowing. You do not belong stuck to the sides of creation. You do belong moving through creation. You are now in this process of becoming unstuck and, as you do, you will become liquid once again. You will no longer feel the need to be stuck to or attached to anyone or anything. You will be in complete harmony with all of creation which then enables you to move through all of creation.

As you learn to move in this fashion you will find it most natural to flow with life. You will not *need* to be stuck to a certain position or even in a certain position on the earth plane. You may begin to travel about and move often or you may begin to find new places to visit and feel the urge to be moving. This is all part of the process of growing unattached. You no longer need the security of your home base, as security is now in you and not outside of you.

You will find that as you begin to become more and more fluid you will more easily shift from position to position or from place to place. You will no longer feel that you must own or hold on to certain positions in order to feel safe and secure. This will eventually lead to giving up ownership of creation. You will no longer *claim* to own parts of the earth or parts of creation. You will no longer wish to own or stick to anything. All will move simply and naturally and all will flow simply and naturally. You will learn to use what is necessary and then allow others to use it. It will not so much be a hand-me-down situation as it will be a sharing. You may need something one day but not the next. Think of it as sharing tools to build a house. You borrow the hammer while your neighbor is using the saw. This will work, as no one will contain a need-to-own-it-all-out-of-fear-of-loss complex. You will all share.

Now, as you begin to know who you are, you will begin to release some of your needs, as they are simply based on fears. So, as you release these needs you begin to see how you could have lived without them in the first place. This allows you to open to the idea that there may be more that you could live without, which begins to free you from little and big areas you are stuck too. You will begin to see how to un-stick by letting go of the idea of needing, and you will begin to realize how you do not necessarily even want all that you believe you need.

As you move into this area of flowing and un-attaching, you will find a new freedom to flow with whatever occurs in your life. You have been programmed to settle down. You have been taught to stay stuck in one place and if you move around too much it is called unstable and that is called bad. It is good. Stop sticking and start moving. Nothing is bad. If you feel the urge to move then do so. How can you be a free spirit if you are living by society's rules that lock you up and prevent you from experiencing all possibilities? You cannot learn to fly by staying in your nest. You may flap your wings and convince yourself that you are moving but you are only moving your wings.

You will find that as you begin to flow with life you may want to stay right where you are and move in the same direction you have always moved in. This too is good. You will know what is good, as all is good and all will feel good. Even those who flap their wings may begin to convince themselves that they are flying, and what you believe is what you are. So, how do you know what is and is not real? It does not matter. Just *allow* all to be possible and by doing so you are not limiting any possibility, you are expanding all possibilities. You are growing and growth is unlimited freedom.

You are in a most advanced state of evolution as you come out of unconsciousness. You are more advanced than you have been in the past and this can cause you to feel as though you are going through big changes. You may even feel physical pain within your body as it stretches and wakes to this new dawning of the light age. As you come out of the dark age and into the light age, your eyes may hurt a little from the shift of dark to light. You may also feel the shift in other areas of your body. Do not get upset. Allow all changes to come and do not fear for your health. You are simply shifting up which is a stretch for you. You are accustomed to shifting down.

You see, as you come into this third dimension you begin immediately to grow and then to shrivel and die. Now you are returning to your growth state in order to allow you to live and ascend. You may even move into a state of accelerated aging in order to speed up your process of letting go of aging. If you see yourself begin to prematurely age in certain areas, you may be confident that this will balance once you have cleared the belief in punishment that caused this symptom. You see, aging is simply a symptom of death. It is not necessary and death is simply an illness. It is nothing more. It is disease that stops the body from functioning properly and it is disease that stops life as you know it.

So; if you begin to see signs in you that you are accelerating towards illness, it may be that you are releasing illness that has been trapped in you for many years. It may also be that you are being prepared to move forward to take on more light. As you move forward to take on more light, you may become content with how you feel and then reach another level of discomfort as you come to another layer of disease and illness. You are layered like an onion and you clear or release your debris as you spin around your cycles. You revolve as does your solar system. You move and you spin at the same time that you pulse or vibrate.

This creates a double action that allows you to revolve in the opposite direction and to spin-off or slough-off everything that you have taken-on. When you begin to reverse spin, you begin to unwind or unravel and let go of whatever you have picked up and are holding. If you are holding a strong belief in aging and death you may feel yourself actually letting go of your hold on death. This takes place on many levels of consciousness and is also felt within your body. So, as you begin to release your hold on death, your body may require extra rest. This is especially true if you are psychic to the extent that you cross dimensions easily.

As you begin to deal with the healing of you, you will begin to doubt. Doubting is your natural state at this point as you are *full* of mistrust and lies. So, as you doubt, you may find yourself getting upset with God for leading you into this mess, which is right here inside of you. Just remember that you created this for a reason and it has a perfect purpose as all does. At this point from where you stand it looks bad, only because you choose bad as a label. In other dimensions there is no bad, so what you call bad simply is.

Now, as you begin to use your body for more than physical gratification, you may begin to experience a shift concerning touching and holding. You may feel as though you do not wish to be touched and holding will become unbearable. This is due in part to the debris that is surfacing and the mistrust that is in you. As you release debris and learn to trust, you will find that you regain trust enough to allow your body to feel touch and to accept touch.

This is also true of the emotional body. It may shut down and release its hold on mistrust and lies, and as it does it may be so overwhelmed by the debris releasing that it will shut down feeling. Feeling is necessary to know yourself and after you have let out enough blocked energy, you will open to feeling once again. In all of this you may feel a great deal of confusion regarding your symptoms. You are simply re-creating you by reversing the system and unwinding what was wound too tightly to you. You are growing by letting go of all that you once were. You are reshaping you and you are re-creating what you once were out of what you have become. You might say that you are creating God out of you.

❧❦

You are beginning to experience the first changes of transformation. These first changes are not necessarily hard to move through. You will develop this ability to change and all new areas of change will occur relatively smoothly. You will be adjusted as you move and you will come out of your stuck position. Little by little you will become more of you with less and less stress and resistance to change. As you become more you, you will begin to realize how you are changing and you may even begin to enjoy this process.

You are at the beginning of your own birth and it is up to you as to how easily you let go of the old and move into the new. You will find that as you become more and more flexible you will become more and more pliable. As you become pliable you are easily taught new ways and you will easily let go of the old. This process will last until you are moving from spirit instead of will. You have been under the control of your will and now spirit is taking over. In such cases you will find it next to impossible to control your life as your *will* dictates, and you will find yourself moving *with* the events that occur in your life. This is spirit moving you. This is being out of control of the will and in the control of spirit. This is being moved and guided and this is being moved to your right place, which may simply be a place where you may take on more of you.

So, as you get moved, be it out of town, out of

relationships, out of a job, or just out of your own area of control, know that you are literally moving out of the will and into spirit. You will no longer be *in control* of your life, or your death, or your birth. You have given up and this is surrender. You are not so much afraid to surrender as you are afraid to give up control in your life. As you give up control you begin to see the benefits. You see, God can give you what you want if you will allow him to. God can take you higher than you have ever been. God is you, and when you *come in,* you will be fully aware of your capabilities and you will begin to take good care of you.

You will no longer feel as though you are being beat up and you will no longer feel the need to punish. You see, God does not punish, God allows. God does not judge, God allows. God is not sin, God is all and you are all. You do not sin so you do not require punishment. You are learning to accept all parts of you and bring them to the light. The light is all. Even darkness is part of the light. Even what you call evil is part of God. It is the part that you twisted and turned around by saying, "This is not God. This is bad and awful and I cannot accept it as God." You left it out of God by not accepting it as God. You made God a limited being by not allowing God to be all things. Now I am asking you to become whole and to begin to accept all of God. Accept all of you. Stop separating God and stop being one way when you can be *all* ways (always).

*I*t will be some time before you actually realize the extent of the change that you are moving into. You will have found certain areas in which you are left with old patterns in order to give you a feeling of security. As you move into greater and greater flexibility, you become more and more aware of the change in your attitude and perception. As you begin to change these, you will begin to see small changes in the physical self. You may begin to sit up straighter or you may begin to like you better and dress you more carefully. You may become a neat clean person or you may find yourself simply thinking you are much better than you once were.

This may be such a subtle shift that you do not actually realize the full extent of the change in you. You may begin to admire how you are creating your life and you may even become proud of who you are. This is very good. You have made pride into a bad thing unless it is given to another. It is acceptable for one to have pride in a child or parent, but you have been taught not to have pride in your own accomplishments. You have been taught that a prideful person is a conceited person, and I want you to know that it is never necessary to put yourself down, or before others, or after others. You are others. They are your reflection of you and they will fall into place as you fall into place.

Each of you are coming into balance and beginning to see how you are all things. If you are all things how can you be afraid to use what is you? If pride is part of you then accept it and allow it to do its job. Each and every part of you has a perfect purpose and, if you *allow* it to be, it will all fall back into balance and begin to do the job it was intended. If you block one emotion you begin to block all emotions. Think of it as a roadblock. If you wish to block off pride, or anger, or hate, you put up a roadblock within you. Now you have love, or peacefulness, or calm driving down this same road and they cannot reach you because you have put up a block to keep out pride and anger. Let them all through. They, like you, are simply passing through. Do not try to control the functions or paths of the emotions. Let them move through you and you will begin to unplug emotionally and come into balance.

At the same time you open to receive anger and hate you will be opening to receive love and peace of mind. All emotions are stopped up in you and this creates a great deal of confusion and panic. Set them free. Let it all be. Allow and accept all parts of you. Do not fight this battle for control of you. You have been strongly convinced to control your emotional body and you have been warned that if you do not you will not be acceptable to society. I am now saying, "Get out of your emotions by letting them go." Let you free! You are trapped in your emotions and you do not know that you are. You are stuck in place holding down that part of you so it will not move.

You are so afraid of your own emotional energy that you have blocked it by placing you in front of it. You are the roadblock. You are the energy that is blocking your own emotional path within you. You put so much energy into this emotional roadblock that you have little to no energy left to love. All your energy goes into prevention instead of preservation. If you would just preserve what you are and accept it as you, you would not have this struggle within you to change you into something you are not. You are not an emotionless being. You have emotion for a reason. You are blocking your flow by trying to shut off part of you and call it bad or dark. Let you be. Allow all of you to be. Stop cutting you up and getting rid of parts you cannot accept.

I want you to begin to accept and embrace all parts of you, even the ones you are coloring dark. What do you know about darkness anyway? You are not even here. You are but a pinpoint of light and from your perspective almost everything looks dark. So, begin to accept you by allowing you to be and, in allowing you to be, you will become more of what you are, and what you are is love and light. Let go of your hold on anger and hatred. It is okay to let it flow. It is not meant to be trapped in you.

⚜

For the first time you are beginning to open. You are like a tiny bud who is just now coming into creation. You are beginning to show your true colors and to burst into view. You are being born as would a tiny seed. First you begin to germinate and then you begin to sprout. You are now in the most important phase of your development which is blooming. You are blooming and when you are all in full bloom you will be so wondrous to see.

You are beginning to see how maybe you do not have all the answers and are leaving yourself open to new possibilities. This leaves you open to all of creation. It makes you available for the Second Coming. This process of becoming is going into its tenth season. It has been upon you now for some time and as you grow into this time of awakening you will begin to discover more of you that you did not know (consciously) existed. You are in a phase of great awakening and great shifting. As you awaken parts of you that have been silent and shut down you may begin to change.

If you find these times a bit hard on you it is only due to the amount of shifting that is necessary to get you *up* to the level you desire. You see, it is all according to you and you will move as directed by you. If you are slower than others it is your choice and if you are faster it is your choice. Do not judge your choices and do not give your power over to those who precede you. You each have your own part to play and each of you has his or her own plan based on his or her capabilities. Let's put it this way. If you were trained to be a technician I would not put you in charge of sewing, and if you were trained to be a seamstress I would not put you in charge of technical engineering. It is all laid out in advance and you each have your position to play in support of the birth of the whole.

The best way to learn your position is to be open and allow yourself to move into situations that are being created by you and for you. You are being guided and even, in some cases, driven to be who you are. For some of you it will fall on your heads as it did with Liane. For others it will be more subtle. Some of you need big action to get your attention. Others will need only a quiet nudge, and still others will need to sleep until the energy is so strong they can no longer find peace in sleep. They will awaken to discover that they have been avoiding what is no longer avoidable, for it will be looking them square in the face.

You can only lie to yourself for so long, and you can only pretend to be asleep, and you can only pretend that God is not on earth now. It is out of this pretending that the truth will emerge. The truth is locked behind the veil and the veil is beginning to part. The truth is God and God is stepping forward to say how creation works, and God is stepping forward to say how you are part of everything and God is stepping forward to say that he is you and you have been deceiving yourselves, and now it is time to wake up to the fact that you create it all and you live in it all.

You are at a point where you will begin to feel shifting within you and this will reflect as big changes outside of you. Know that as you view your choices you will know that everything is perfect and on schedule. Do not worry that you are becoming an uncaring insensitive person. You are not. You are simply letting go of judgment and without judgment there is no big upset, and no big excitement, and no overwhelming of the emotional body. Without judgment there is simply the seeing of the situation and the knowledge that all is well. There is never any reason to be upset and never any reason to shake up the emotions.

You will find that as you move deeper and deeper into love and higher and higher out of fear, you will be navigating in new waters of creative ability, and you may create your life from a much higher perspective with no need to cling to others or cling to anything. You will be riding high and free of needs and emotional distress. You will be fearless instead of fearful. You will know you can trust you and you will be in love with you. The greatest gift you can give you is to be in love with you. You are God.

꧁꧂

As long as you are in the dormant phase you have no recollection of just who you are. As you begin to move from dormant into growth, you begin to sprout and realize new parts of yourself. You will find that not only are you beginning to grow, you are also beginning to take on light. This light that you take on is sometimes disturbing for you in that light is trust and faith. Light is wisdom and knowledge and awareness that you are being moved into position and not simply being pushed and shoved around. As you begin to understand movement, you will begin to understand how certain situations and certain individuals are drawn into your life to act as a catalyst to ignite you or move you. As you begin to see how this works you will begin to let go of your use of the term victim. You are never pushed or shoved without consent. You must consent on some level or you would not draw the situation nor the person who pushes and shoves. Sometimes it is as simple as pushing you out of a situation you wish to take root in or stick to. Sometimes, when you wish to stick to something, you draw someone or some situation to move you on so you will not get stuck where you do not belong.

This is catalysis and it is good. You move you by moving someone else or something else up against you. Sometimes you are the pusher, and it is you who have been drawn by another to create a catalytic force to move either, or both, of you along. As you begin to understand these forces, you will begin to understand how you are creating all that you see. This is why I tell you to run if the situation does not feel good. Some situations are created to get you to move, but you have become so addicted to pain that you stay and continue to take on more and more pain.

I want you to be free. I want you to know that you have free will and that you choose where you will stay and where you will not stay. You choose based on your feelings, and right now feelings are not sending the proper signals, based on how much or how little pain you carry. As you begin to clear feelings by allowing them to move and be felt by you, you will begin to know you and to know your free will choices. Right now, you choose and you do not realize what you choose or how you choose. You are a dysfunctioning computer who is spewing out the same misinformation you have always been programmed to repeat. Now we are changing your programming and building a new system that will carry you forward with ease and move you out of struggle.

The war is over! It is time for peace and this peace begins right here inside of you. You are beginning to see how you create all the stuff you do not appreciate and now you will learn to either appreciate or let-go-of and move on to better for yourself. You are moving into free will and out of a force of will. You are moving into balance and out of imbalance. You are becoming all that you are which is multifaceted instead of one sided. You are beginning to see all possibilities as good and all possibilities as real. You are beginning to shift from narrow vision to expanded vision.

You are now in a position to begin to accept what you feel and to trust what you feel. You will no longer defend your logic when you know in your heart that another truth exists. You will no longer be an extremist when you know you can get there with ease. You will no longer push at you to be better when you know that your perception of what is better is simply a perspective or point of view. In actuality, what you are beginning is a phase of seeing and knowing without being told and, sometimes, in spite of what you are told. You will begin to see the truth and will no longer depend on hearing the truth.

Your truth will become apparent, as will the lies. You will become more and more transparent, as will those you interact with. This is the waking up; the seeing, the knowledge that all is and always has been just as planned. Nothing will excite you as nothing will be a surprise. Nothing will be worth getting upset over as nothing will hold undue importance for you. You will move when the catalyst moves you and you will stay when you are not moving. No big deal. No big reasons for moving or staying. You are simply passing through and *enjoying* the ride.

꧁꧂

You may find that you no longer wish to be hurt and you no longer wish to seek revenge on yourself for past sins. As you begin to clear your need for punishment you will begin to release your hold on revenge. All revenge is self-revenge just as all hate is self-hate and all judgment is self-judgment. When you learn to set yourself free you will no longer feel the need to punish you or the perpetrator who you believe is responsible for making your life miserable.

As you get to a point of self-realization you will become quite aware that you are creating and using your catalyst to perform your deeds for you. You are punishing you by creating a situation that you do not like because you believe you must repent or "pay for" your sins. You need not repent and you need not "pay for." You are "free." You may choose to be and do whatever you choose from your own "free will." You do not come into the world of free will to be punished for using your free will. You do not need to be hurt and to suffer.

Stop believing in sin and stop believing in right and

wrong. There is no right and there is no wrong. You are here to learn to be "free" spirits, not to be restricted and punished for your choices. If you make a choice that causes pain or restriction of movement you will simply back up and go in a new direction. You are not to be extracting revenge on yourself and forcing yourself into constant uncomfortable situations just because you believe you once sinned; and now you are believing you are tired of pain and I wish to show you how you create it all. If you have revenge thoughts towards another it is your reflection of seeking revenge upon yourself. You may wish to leave this person so he or she will feel bereft in your absence. This too is a form of revenge. You take you as far away as possible, and do not respond to that individual again as if you did not exist for him or her. This, of course, is only one way of dealing out revenge. There are many ways of getting back at others and many ways of seeking revenge on another.

As you begin to learn how you can only think what you already carry in you, you will begin to learn how you are clearing your own belief system in order to take on a whole new belief system, that will raise you to a much higher level of consciousness. Most of what you believe concerning right and wrong was taught to you on this plane and it will keep you on this plane. What you are learning now is coming from the next dimension and beyond to even the next. You will find that you are literally being pulled up into the fourth and fifth dimensions. You are shifting consciousness in order to arrive in these dimensions and you need not go anywhere except into you to travel.

This is ascension. This is the movement forward, the movement upward, the movement into the light. You are leaving behind what you once were and taking on the light in expanded form to give you expanded vision. You are God arriving in matter. You are matter, as you were sent ahead to prepare the way. It all came from the whole that is you and it will all go back to the whole that is you. You are you and God is you. God is arriving in you to create more of you from what he is. You are still being created which means that God is re-creating God. God is shifting to one side of himself to allow an opening for more of himself. When God shifts back to the other side he will take this side into the light with him. He is big and he holds a lot.

You may find that as you begin to release revenge to the light, it will begin to disappear and you will be left with only choices without punishment for choosing. As this becomes evident, you will begin to make much broader choices, as you will know that you will no longer find bad choices, or punishment, at the end attached to the choice. You will no longer need to protect yourself as your need to punish you will have fled with your need to seek revenge. You will simply make your mistakes and say, "Oops! I'd best go another direction," and that will be that. No attached pain to linger into resentment, to grab on to anger, to seek repayment for a debt you believe you owe. It will be finished in the blink of an eye. It will be no more powerful than "oops!"

You will now begin to change and you will now begin to become light. As you begin these changes your body functions will also change. You will no longer require your body to do certain aspects of work that you have required in the past. The body will begin to take on a new life, and part of that new life may begin with rebellion. Your body may begin to act on its own and refuse to follow the will. The will has been in charge for eons and now that it is merging with spirit it is no longer in control. Will power has lost its will to survive and is now being replaced with love power.

The will to live may also leave you and you will be left without the need to struggle so much to stay alive. You will begin to flow, which means that you will be open to life or death and you all know by now that it is all the same thing. So, as you begin to see how you are letting go of struggle and strong denial, you will begin to see how you do not always have control of you. You will begin to understand what you are so afraid of, and what you are so afraid of is losing control. You are not so afraid of losing your life as you are afraid of not being in control.

How can you possibly allow God to take over if you will not let go of control? How can you possibly allow the part of you who is creator in if you will not give up your hold on you? How can you possibly allow God to reign in you if you will not allow you to step down from your control box? You have not done well with this mission and now it is time to admit that the reason you have not done well is because you are not all here. Now is the time of arrival. You are seeping back into you in a very slow, monotonous fashion and you are discovering your true nature which is not struggle and war, but peace and joy.

As you begin to uncover your true nature, you will also see that you are becoming so much more than you ever expected. You are becoming alive with truth and light and this too affects change within your body. The truth will set you free of the old ways and old restraints. The truth will allow you to move into an entirely new area of clearing and releasing. As you clear and release you may feel a bit weak. You see, you are clearing your own discarded belief system and it is so old that it is putrefied. It has begun to decay and, as it leaves your system, it may stir up some unpleasant side effects. You may sneeze a great deal and you may get weak, dizzy, faint or just plain ill. The level of illness depends on the amount of debris that is evacuating the system at any given moment.

When you begin to feel ill, try to remember that your body has been poisoned for so long that now it is uncomfortable without your constant poisoning. You are in a state of preparing for ascension and fine tuning your vehicle. You no longer slough off your body, you transform your body. Body is what it's all about. You travel in it and experience through it. You will wish to know that with proper maintenance your body will go on forever. It was created to be flexible and to last. It was also created to be your best friend. Do you treat your body like your best friend? Do you hug it and give it only the best nutrition and maintenance, or do you poison it with chemicals and toxins and alcohol and nicotine? You are in charge of you. You keep God in you. How have you done as the keeper of God?

∿⁘

As long as you are becoming this new you, you may as well enjoy it. Learn to embrace all parts of you so that you no longer fight with you. You can learn to embrace all parts of you by allowing all that you do to be okay. Do not push at you and do not push away parts of you that frighten you. Most of you are afraid of your anger and you push it away. I want you to look at it and feel it. It is you. Anger is simply an emotion, an expression of the self. It must be allowed to move in you and through you to be released.

As you release, you begin to create a vacuum and this vacuum will be filled with the acceptance that was given to the anger. So, as you accept all parts of you, you begin to create love for all of you. You will find that as this love grows, you will grow with it. As love dissolves anger and hatred you will feel the benefits. As you begin to send love and acceptance to all parts of you, you allow you to know that you are lovable and acceptable, and eventually you become what you are which is loving acceptance.

As you move from the darkness into thelight, you may find it difficult to be who you once were. You may find that you no longer feel the need to get upset over situations that once were so distressing to you. You will find that balance is coming into your life and it is no longer necessary to protect yourself by your anger. You will let go of your need to get angry and feel hurt, as you will be learning to move anger into love. You are learning to turn everything into love as love is all there really is.

As you begin to move all into love, you may find that you are moving into love. Loving acceptance allows all to be good and all to be lovable. You will find that you are most lovable when you love all of you and allow all of you to be. This will draw to you new images in your giant reflections and these images will be allowing and accepting to the degree that you are allowing and accepting. You will also find that you may become quite fond of who you are and you may begin to have very loving thoughts concerning your being and who you are.

This is good. This is love and this is self-love. You will find that as you learn to love yourself, you will be in a very good place. You will find it difficult to think from logic as you once did, as most logic taught you to "get real" and to get real is basically to allow for pain instead of pleasure. You have been taught to not be dreamers and now it is time to let go of pain and move into the dream. The dream is more accurate than the reality you have come to regard as real. Dream! Dream very big beautiful dreams and know that they too serve a purpose and they too have their place in creation.

Once you have learned to not "get real" and to stay in your fantasy world, you may actually create it. You may believe strongly enough, for long enough, that it totally and illogically takes the place of reality. Once it has transcended the logic and moved into imagination anything is possible. Absolutely anything can be created when enough juice is given to create and the juice does not have to bounce off all the old programming that says, "I must punish me for my sins." This clearing of punishment, and your belief *in* bad and evil, will allow you to *release* your hold on the *idea* that you need to be put in your place and controlled, so that you will no longer sin. Then, as you move out of your need to be held down and punished, you may move up into creative joy and know that "creation is yours to do with as you wish!"

You are at the beginning of a new dawn. You are beginning to see how you will become the creator and how you are the creation. As you create more and more, you will begin to see new realities evolve out of old realities. You will begin to see the layering of dimensions and you will begin to see how you create from a system of materialization of energy. As you learn how you create, you will begin to un-create what is no longer necessary for today's new belief in reality. As you believe so you create; and as you create so you believe. Once you have moved into a state of total trust and faith you will no longer find it necessary to believe in certain restrictions, and these restrictions will begin to fade from your created realities.

Some of you restrict yourselves from joy, and some of you restrict yourselves from peace, and still others restrict yourselves from total love and acceptance of all. Do you accept all? Can you accept that you are God and that you contain all that God is? Can you handle that God is omnipresent and oversees all that is? Can you handle that God allows all to occur and how you are this God? Can you handle that you do not love you out of choice? And can you handle that you are also becoming love out of choice?

There are no unplanned events there are only unforeseen events. You may plan for and receive but you do not necessarily know all that went into the preparation to carry out the plan. If you are creating from love then love will motivate the plan. If, on the other hand, you are creating from unresolved fear, you will be motivated by fear and the plan will be a fearful or fear-filled plan. If you decide to allow all to be, you allow fear to move over or maybe merge with love to transform into love. In this case you can allow love and fear to work together in order to become one. Fear will always dissolve into love, as the dark determines shadows and the light allows shadows to move into light.

So, as you do your creating, you may begin to

create new realities over your old realities, and these new realities will actually dissolve away the old. The memory of hurt and pain can literally be wiped away with love and acceptance. As you create from this new you, you will create right over some of the old you and this new you will begin to take over and dissolve away the old. It is a sort of reality layering that causes you to move in a new direction. More and more layers are required to create this new reality from the old. This is transforming one reality into another.

As you learn how you create these realities you will feel yourself slip back into old programs and old patterns. This could be a point where two realities or layers are being formed into one. This could be the old you dissolving into the new you and you may experience it as a slipping of sorts. Do not worry. You are not going back you are going forward. As you begin to feel these movements more and more, you will become aware that change is taking place in you and you *are* this change that is taking place. You are reality and you are the creator of your reality. So, if you feel you've changed, you are also feeling reality change.

The great shift is on. You are shifting into God and God is dissolving you. You are becoming one with "all that is;" and "all that is," is the totality of conscious and unconscious reality. You are becoming and you are realizing or becoming real. This is God becoming real. This is God realizing his potential through the many cells at once. This is the tuning-in to God and the waking up to the realization that you are God. You are all that is and you are now learning who you are.

As you begin to receive more and more light, it will

be easier and easier to bring forth the darkness that you have buried in you. As it becomes easier to bring it forth, it will bubble to the surface in larger and larger bubbles of dark energy. Once you have faced and accepted your darkness you can then dissolve it and re-create it into whatever you like. You name the game as you always have. In the past your game was good vs. evil. Now it may be something new like "peace on earth." Yes! This is a good title for your next game here on earth.

≪⚜≫

You have begun ascension and are rising, within yourself, to a fourth and fifth dimensional perspective. Peace, love and brotherhood are all a state of mind as are heaven and hell. As you become all that you are meant to be, you will be rising faster and faster. As you rise more quickly you will feel the pull of the three-dimensional world that you are leaving behind. It may not feel so much like you are rising. It may, at times, feel more like you are sinking, or falling backward in production of your lives. You are not.

Sometimes it takes two steps backward before you can assess the situation and figure out how best to move forward. You will not always understand why certain situations and events are occurring in your life but, eventually, you will see all as good and right. Everything happens in accordance with the master plan and the master plan is part of you. As you begin to see how you have become part of the plan, I wish you to remember that you are still in body. Take good care of your body. Your body will allow you to become all that you are more easily and effortlessly. Your body remembers and can be your greatest gift. Your body is not a cumbersome machine that is in your way. It is how you operate within this particular dimension and it is very helpful indeed.

So, help your body by being kind to you. Love you and care for you and be sure to feed and water you well. Do not overfeed and do not underfeed. Be of good cheer and know that a happy body is a happy memory bank. The body carries all cellular memory and can be of great service to you. For those of you who constantly push your body to strive for perfection, I suggest you ease up and allow body to determine its own growth and healing. Sometimes, in the same way that you will get upset and rebel when pushed at constantly, your body will get upset and rebel when pushed at constantly.

Body has a way of dealing with healing and cellular change. You are in the midst of great cellular change and you may see your body rush forward and age before you see it transform to youth. Your body is being prepared by you to be inhabited by you. You are returning to a state of total awareness and with this state of awareness comes a certain amount of releasing and shifting within your body. As this shifting begins to take place you may find yourself manifesting certain symptoms that you would not ordinarily have. You may literally release blocked energy that may have created serious illness in your distant future. In such cases, you may begin to experience parts of the illness without really getting sick.

At these times I wish you to know that you are simply clearing and releasing old pent-up energy that is surfacing now to save you from illness later on. You are beginning to rise up out of your belief in death, and illness is simply a symptom of death, since death is simply an illness in itself. So remember, sometimes it's two steps back to assess the damage, and oftentimes a little cleaning up and cleaning out before we move forward with new construction.

࿇

As you begin to realize how you are creating your reality, you will become more flexible with your choices. You will no longer insist on having everything this way or that way. You will begin to understand how everything has a time and everything has a place. Nothing is by accident and nothing is out of place. Each time you find something wrong in your life I wish you to look at what it may be teaching you on a power level. Power is where you live. You are not weak and to surrender is not weak.

You will find that as you continue this ascension process you will continue to let go of your fears and insecurities. If you lose something it is simply to show you how you are powerful enough to live without whatever it is that you were holding on to for dear life. As you see how you do not fall apart when you have let go of the big material weights, you will see how creative you really are. You are adaptable and changeable and flexible. This is how you were created. You were meant to be molded not to be hard and rigid and *set* in your ways. As you begin to move and flow you begin to create anew. It is only in the movement that creation is moved. As you move so moves your creation. If you are set and unmoving your creation will be set and unmoving.

If you want change I suggest you start by changing you. You are the one who shifts or does not shift. You are the one who creates it all. You are the one who is viewing your creation and if you wish to see a flexible, loving creation then you must become flexible and loving. Whatever you are is what you reflect out and receive back. So, as you go about your daily life I wish you to really look at what you create and really own it. If you refuse to own what you create you refuse to own all of it, not just the parts you deny.

As you become more and more generous about accepting and owning your reality you will become more and more generous about accepting all parts of you, which allows you to become whole that much sooner. So, do not push away what you create. Allow it to show you who you are and then it will move on, as you shift to a new level just from viewing how you are as opposed to how you wish to be. When you look at a reflection and see how it is reflecting to you, you will be able to see a part of you. If you do not like the reflection you do not like this part of you. Now you may change this part of you and allow yourself to shift into a new level of awareness concerning how you have always been, without realizing that you were.

Some of you act pretty silly most of the time, and it is entirely possible that you have no idea how you look to the rest of the world. If you had a camera follow you around day in and day out you would get the idea. You have little discrepancies in your nature and you often contradict yourself just to prove how right you are. You all exaggerate your way through many a conversation, just to make it look as though you were the good guy while the others in your stories couldn't compare to you. It is time to tell the truth. Any experience you have ever had with anyone in your life was a direct experience with yourself.

Now you have to figure out who you are and why you make up stuff, or just distort it to make you look good. No one tells a story with the intent of making themselves look like the villain. Did you ever notice how there are always two sides and usually they are exact opposites? Then, of course, there are all the positions in between. It is as if you are creating an opposing view, when you could have the same view with all other possibilities thrown in. When you don't want to be the same as, out of distaste for, you can make two apples look like opposites. When you are so into judgment and competition, you can create competition. Also, when you are into being free of conflict you can find something to agree on. You can always find common ground if you wish to.

You will find that the more you look for the

common ground the less difficulty you will have in agreeing on creation. Sometimes you can simply agree on the ability to agree. You are taught to stand up and fight for your rights and this is creating confusion. Not all of you wish for the same things, so it is best to allow each individual to be and to grow without restricting them in anyway. This is not easy for you to do. You have a very difficult time allowing freedom and this is why you do not see freedom in your own world. You have rules and regulations and "Big Daddy is always watching so you'd better not do anything illegal." When you begin to allow others the freedom to be who they are, you will begin to see a new freedom in your own life. Remember, there is no right or wrong, there only is.

∝⟐⟐

You are as vulnerable to the light as you are to the dark. The only difference being that you are more accustom to the dark. You will learn that as you give up your need to twist light you will begin to see clearly. If you have a need to be punished for past sins, you may find it quite simple to turn any situation into a bad or unhappy situation. This is due to the energy that you are putting into your own demise, due to your past belief that you have sinned and must be punished. It is due to your belief that all bad things are punished to free the soul and make things "right" again.

You even carry guilt if you do not get punished, and often you create great illness and often death from this guilt that you carry. This guilt is due to the belief in wrong and it is in you because you bought into it. It is part of you because you swallowed it hook, line and sinker. It is you! You have become what you believe, and often what you believe is killing, or, at the very least, punishing you. You will find that when you let go of guilt, you let go of your need to punish you. You let go of your belief that you are not a nice person and you let go of your belief that you are a crook or schemer who got away with something that you should not have.

Let go of guilt and begin to allow all to be acceptable and you will become acceptable. You need not be punished for your sins because you did not sin. Sin was created to distract you into the darkness and it has worked quite effectively. Come home to the light. It is your true color. You are God and you do not require forgiveness nor do you require punishment. You are a child of God and you need not be scolded, nor trained, to be a good boy/girl or a bad boy/girl. You are born into love and nothing can make you unlovable except your own denial of love.

You may begin to conquer your own denial of love by allowing yourself to receive only good. Know that you are receiving good and allow all to be acceptable. You make all choices regarding the directions you take and your higher good is working for you. Do not judge situations as bad. See all as something good to learn and grow from. Move on when it is most important and stay when it is most important. You will begin to learn from instinct how to evaluate your growth and it is good to trust you enough to trust your own instinct. As you grow closer and closer to the light you will begin to see how the light is not harmful and situations are not harmful. You are being given what was created out of a belief in right and wrong, or good and bad. Now that you are learning to come out of this game of good vs. evil, you will wish to allow all to be seen as simply energy moving into and out of your life.

As you allow the flow of energy to merge and return you will begin to see the most remarkable changes take place. You will begin to see love where you never thought it existed and you will begin to see a good and right purpose for creation. You will begin to see how you distorted the truth in order to get "into" this dimension, and how now that you are in you all want out. You will begin to see how it is not this dimension you want out of so much, as it is the distortion that you hate. The distortion is what is killing you and it will soon disappear into the light of truth. As the distortion disappears you will become whole, as you will be allowed to *see* the rest of you for what you are and not for what the distortion has presented you to be.

This is the uncovering of you, the digging out of you. You are buried beneath all the garbage that was heaped on you to keep you down, but without this garbage you would have floated right out of here. So I guess the biggest question is, "Why on earth would you come here if you knew you had to be held down to gain a foothold?" This is God going into all areas of creation in order to know and accept his creation. God felt movement and wanted to know who he is. He sent his only son or a part of himself. He reproduced and sent more of himself out into the darkness to know what it was. Is it all God or is it another? This is the simplest way to put it for where you are now. It is God wanting to see all parts of God.

✿

You are the most flexible and adaptable creature in this creation. You have simply hidden the fact that you are. You scream and shout how unjust it is to do this or that to a human and yet, if you could *realize* the truth, you would see that no injustice could truly affect you without your agreement. As you learn to use your abilities for advancement, you will learn how you are an advanced race with capabilities beyond your present recognition.

You are coming to a place in your history where you will begin to uncover your darkest secrets, and maybe some of your power held secrets. You have utilized certain powers in the past, but you shut them down due to your inability to stabilize your own center of awareness. Now that you are moving into a new level of awareness you may find it most interesting to uncover what your capabilities hold. You are moving into a time of great awakening and, as you do, you may become aware of certain abilities, or areas of power to heal, or maybe to transform objects, or just to *feel* certain events as or before they occur.

All of these abilities are part of you and have always been. You are simply awakening and so are they. They lie dormant in you just as you do. They are part of you and, as you begin to heal and awaken, you may find yourself beginning to re-experience some of these abilities. As you do so you may begin to play with these energies and to enjoy this part of creation. Do not feel the need to go into denial over ownership of any powers you may awaken. It is not necessary to declare that God gave you this or that, as you are God and God declares only that all is. To assume that you must declare that God is working through you, if you heal another, is the same as to assume that God is working through you when you make a touchdown so you must give the credit to God.

Give up this silly need to feel that God only works through good people doing good things. God works in and through and is everyone doing everything. As you begin to realize how you are God, you will not make such a big deal out of such little things. As you begin to realize how you are God, waking up to the idea that you are, you will begin to accept you and all parts of you more readily. It is not often that you really know who you are and it will be offered to you in many ways. You will begin to see yourself create in many ways and you will begin to awaken in many ways.

This is all part of the process of knowing God. It is the knowing and the awareness and the light that will allow you to own you. You are in denial coming forward to face the truth. The truth is that "God lives," and "God lives" because you live. Does that sound like it is backward to you? It is perhaps forward and you are a little mixed up and backward.

You will not find God outside of you. You will find him right inside where he has always been and you will find that he has been patiently waiting, for a very long time, for you to grow up and be God.

❧

*F*or as long as there has been creation there has been light. There has been a certain amount of darkness only out of necessity to keep the light at a distance. You had a problem receiving the light from the beginning. It is due to the immense energy buildup surrounding your world. In the beginning *all* was light. There became a time, however, that the light was too strong and it affected many in an adverse way. The light then became a thing to fear and it was shunned by those who could not retain it without fear of it. It became a thing to fear and it was "pushed out" and "put up above" where it could not affect those who did not wish to deal with it directly.

This became a time of godlessness or darkness. This was a time when all mankind would learn to deny the light in favor of the darkness which, at that time, was more acceptable. It has become evident to mankind that light is necessary to sustain balance. It is an important part of humankind and it is an important part of the individual cells that make up any living organism. You, as humans, may be a living, breathing, thinking cell, however, you still have a great deal to learn about survival and life.

You are not the most intelligent species to ever inhabit this or any other planet. There have been many others with varying degrees of intelligence, and they have conquered many lands and developed their physical skills and abilities to a fine degree. None, however, have had the opportunity that is placed before you. No other civilization has been allowed to grow into God and allow God to "become" in a new form by transmuting the energy that "is" into what it will "be." This new opportunity is why so many are on earth at this time. It is a unique opportunity, for those who wish to give birth to God, to do so. It is a time of healing the old in order to make room for the new. It is a time of growth in order to release and become less of what you have always been.

And what have you always been? It is widely known that you are in denial as a species. You have been the only species to successfully deny its own genetic makeup. You call what you cannot describe as useful to you, within the individual body, "junk." Junk DNA is not junk. How much of this junk DNA do you have? Is it ninety percent as with the portion of your brain that you do not use? You have shut down ninety percent of you and now is the time of awakening and re-opening to give birth to the light of truth. Allow you to be all that you can be by allowing God to be all that he can be. Do not be afraid my child. When you step into a new area that is dark and frightens you, allow yourself the knowledge and wisdom that God is in you, and you are actually God and have created all that is occurring for a very good reason.

Trust! Trust! Trust! I do not mean trust that if you wish to learn something you will do it perfectly the very first time. I do mean trust that you can and trust that you may do even more in your future. You are just now stretching and feeling the body. It is as though a stone statue of a man or woman has come alive. You have entered it and are now learning to make it move in the direction you choose. You must be patient with this newly risen body. It is not accustomed to flexibility and movement. It was stuck in one position for a very long time.

***

You are about to become the most miraculous part of your own self. This is the part of you that has not been allowed to surface for many, many years. You might say it has been dormant since life, as you know it, began. This is the part of you who will know what to do and will not need to be taught. This is the part of you that will allow you to love you and to nurture life within you. This is the part of you that is not only light; it is the beginning of the beginning.

You will find that as you rise you will be allowed to view more and more of what is available to the human species. As you rise you will be told, by your own inner knowing, how you will direct your future and how you will each accomplish your own salvation. You will learn that you do not know who you are now, as it is best to arrive in drips and dabs, sort of like a faucet that is dripping into a pail unnoticed. But look how quickly the pail can fill to overflowing without ever being noticed. This will be you. You will flow with fluid and liquid movement. You will no longer be stone; you will be melting and flowing into and around creation. You will no longer be separate from God and you will no longer be separate from creation.

You are learning to be liquid and you are learning to penetrate the third dimension in order to change it into a much better place. You will saturate and infiltrate until there is nothing left untouched by God. God is entering, and it is you God is entering and it is you God is becoming. You are the true creator of this universe and you created all that you see. You are the one who busily created the stars and planets and even evolution. You created it all and now you are entering and becoming what you have created. You are the greatest being who has ever been and you find yourself so hard to live with and love, at times, that it is difficult to keep you *in* you.

You all want out! You want out of you and into someone else or to be put someplace else. What you do not realize is that your darkness is what you really want out of. You will find that when you come out of the darkness you will be a little confused and even lost. You have become so adapted to and addicted to darkness that to be light will feel wrong. It will not feel right at times and it will not feel comfortable. I wish you to remember that you are becoming the most magnificent being and it is with care and love that you are being taken-over. Your true identity is coming in and will leave no stone unturned in this process of bringing you to the light. This can mean discomfort on certain levels as you begin to show your dark its *way* and lead it gently into the light so that it may be exposed and healed. Your body can endure and will come out on top. Not only will your physical body come out on top, it will also transform into its potential for freedom and compliance, all with perfect balance.

You will transform completely and totally into the light of God. You will see all that is possible with God and all that is meant to be perfect. You will know love as you have never before and you will experience it in a body. Love is and love does, but never before has love entered form and totally absorbed and transformed the fear that is built up and stored within the cellular structure. Love is being born and will take over until there is no fear left to fear. You'll become total love and light. You will become whole and complete. You will want for nothing and you will emanate all that is holy. This is your future. This is who and what you are. You are literally the light and the love of this world.

I believe you are beginning to see how you will not only feel like a new person; you will literally become a new person. In this process of transformation you must be allowed to adjust to all new growth, and the best way to allow you to adjust is to give you time in between spurts of growth. This time will allow you to heal and to settle in your new and latest level achieved. You are currently seeking peace of mind and this too will be achieved.

As you begin to develop more and more of your capabilities, you will begin to see how you are not only 'not' hurting yourself by your growth, you are actually assisting your development and your reason for being here. When you plant seeds, you will find that some sprout and some do not, some come up in early spring while others wait until fall before they have the strength to burst forth. This, of course, depends on climate and on location and on watering and sun hours. There are many factors that determine the growth of plant life just as there are many factors that determine the growth of you.

You are in a position now to become one of the most wondrous of blooms. Your only job is to grow. You must, however, nurture and supply light to your own growth and development. You will become a plant who sends out long roots to find food and water. You will draw to you the people and information that is needed to assist you in your growth and development. You are self-sufficient and you will be taught, by you, what works for your growth and what does not. It is all up to you and it is all your choice. Trust your choice and know that you will do whatever is best for you. Trust that you are divinely guided and that every occurrence in your life has a purpose. Sometimes it is just a small purpose, yet it is there for a reason.

You will find that as you develop more and more trust toward your own self, you will become closer to your own self. You will also come to know who you are and to know who you are becoming. As you develop into this new being that you are now in the process of becoming, you will grow more and more tired of your old ways and less and less tolerant of them. Eventually, you will let them go and develop a whole new way of seeing all that is.

This is transformation. This is letting go of the old in order to become the new. You are being born out of the old. You are taking you and growing into you while you still exist in you. You might say, you are adding more of you to make you twice what you are. Then, when you can tolerate your own brilliance, you will become even more. And this will continue until you have become so much of you that you have no room for fear, or anything else that has been working in you and through you.

All will disappear and all will fall by the wayside. No pain, no illness, no longing to be more because you will have become all that is and all that you are. These are glorious and wondrous times and much is happening within creation and within God. It is a time of germination and it is the time of letting go of smallness and becoming vast indeed. No more petty disease and no more petty thoughts. No more petty brilliance. We are moving into a time of true brilliance and total acceptance of what is. No more small minds when you can develop the biggest, broadest mind with dual perception.

You are moving into the greatest time in created history. You are becoming God simply by stretching you big enough to hold the thought that you are God, and God is all therefore you are all. As you begin to move into a state of extended grace, you will move through life with grace. You will be trusting, and with trust comes faith and faith dances with grace. You will be most joyous as you reach this level of grace, and you will truly flow with all of life and you will not find it necessary to argue or debate anything, as nothing will have just one side.

You are moving and evolving and taking on the most wonderful changes. Some may not feel good at first, but once you settle into the new thought, the new belief, you will adjust nicely and then you will grow that much bigger and broader in the mind area. To be broad-minded in all situations is a very good place to be. How broad-minded are you and how much broader do you believe you can get?

ॐ

Now is the time to become whole. You have never been incomplete and you do not have part of you missing. All parts are in place. You must learn to *accept* all parts as you. You must learn to know all parts as you and you must learn to receive all parts as you. No more denial. It is all you. Everything you create is for you and everything you do not create is out of wisdom. Allow yourself to start right here where you are today and to allow yourself to be wisdom. Allow yourself to know the difference between light and what you call dark. Allow yourself to know that in the same way that you all judge an artist's work as stupid and ugly one century – and then out of nowhere in the next century you begin to go "ooh" and "ah" over it and exclaim its beauty and wonder – you all *decide* what to judge.

You are all changing all of the time and you decide, or judge, what is black and what is white. You have the ability within your own self to make everything okay. You don't have to judge it as black or white. You can simply *allow* it to be acceptable and know that it has merit even though you can't see its merit from where you now stand. You will soon shift your position and then you will be able to see better. Your view is simply blocked at this time and those blocks are what we are clearing.

This is a very good time to suggest love. I want you to love you and to get to know you. You are pretty wonderful and well worth knowing. As you learn more and more about your true identity and as you bring to the surface some of your diseased beliefs, you may find it difficult to accept you. You will know when you have reached this level of clearing your debris, as you will draw to you what you are clearing. If you are clearing your fear of rejection you will create situations whereby you will *feel* rejected. It need not be a true situation of rejection, but you will color it as rejection because you have brought your fear of rejection to the surface.

This is how clearing works. You bring it up and it expresses itself as it comes forward. Everything simply needs to express in order to heal. Then, once it is healing, it will begin to give off signals. You will feel more rejection, and gradually it will disappear and you will be left with no feeling of rejection by anyone or anything.

You have taught yourself to know only what you wish to in order to protect yourself. You are now moving into an area of complete trust and faith. This draws grace into your life. With grace you literally glide through life and the struggle disappears. Know that you are all moving towards grace and know that you will soon find your way through your own self created darkness into the light that has always been you. You are a child of light and you have simply shut down in order to achieve a certain level of grounding within this dimension. Now it is time to tune in and turn on to full capacity so that you may raise this entire dimension to the next.

Do you remember the story I told you about the ship lost at sea and sunk on the ocean floor? And how the rescue was at hand and we would fill this submerged vessel with a giant balloon, and pump this balloon to full capacity and float the ship to the surface? This balloon is you. Part of you came to rescue you. You are being insulated with love and light now. We could not have submerged the balloon fully inflated because, for one thing, an inflated balloon goes up not down, for another, you are too "big" in your insulated state. We had to deflate the light out of you to get you to earth. Now you are here and you have grown quite accustom to the heavy atmospheric pressure, and now you are being *put in place* in order to raise this entire dimension once you are pumped back up with light.

You are in charge. You are doing all of this. You are here on a mission and in order to come on this mission it was necessary to deflate. Now this is changing, so do not judge the change and do not judge the technique that brought you here. You offered to help. It is all your choice, your free will.

We will discuss more of what you came here to do in our next book. For now, know that you are God doing God's work. Every last one of you has his or her part to play, so don't discount your ability nor your role in this.

God's Pen

I first heard the voice of God in 1988. I was sitting in my back yard reading a book when this big booming voice interrupted with, "I am God and I will not come to you by any other name." I felt like the voice was everywhere – inside of me as well as in the sky around me. I was so frightened that I ran in my bedroom to hide.

This was not the first time that I heard voices. I had been communicating with my own spirit guide or soul for about a year. I guess my depth of fear regarding God, and all that he represented to me at the time, was just too much.

I spent two days trying to avoid the voice of God, which was patiently waiting for me to respond. By the second day I was exhausted from lack of sleep and decided to give in and talk with him. This turned out to be the greatest gift and best decision of my life.

The first book, *God Spoke through Me to Tell You to Speak to Him*, shows my evolution from communicating with my soul to communicating with the Big Guy. It took a couple years for me to be comfortable communicating with God. My fear of a punishing God was big! That has most definitely changed and I now think of God as my partner and best friend.

In the beginning the voice of God would wake me in the middle of the night and tell me it was time to write. He said I had promised to do this work (I assumed he was talking about the soul/spirit me). I would drag myself up to a sitting position and watch in amazement as my hand flew across the page, while I tried to keep up by reading what was being written.

It was always so much fun to wake up the next morning and grab my notebook to see what God had written during the night. After some time the voice stopped waking me and I became comfortable picking up my pen and writing for God first thing in the morning. I think in the beginning I had to be awakened while still semi-conscious from sleep so I wouldn't object too much to the information that was being channeled through me.

As I grew less and less afraid (and more trusting) of God, he was able to communicate greater information. Some of the information is quit controversial, but I felt it important to just let it be and not censor it. I present the writings here to you as they were given to me. I have edited a little (mostly the more personal information regarding myself) and I have used a pen name for privacy reasons. I asked God for a good pen name and he guided me to Liane which (I was told) in Hebrew means "God has answered."

At one point I became a little concerned about my sanity in all this, so I went to a hypnotherapist to find out what I was doing. Under hypnosis I saw this incredibly huge beam of light with a voice coming from within it. It was a giant "loving light" and felt so comforting and kind. It felt like that's where I came from. After that I stopped worrying about my sanity. If this is crazy, I think it's a very good kind of crazy to be….

In loving light, Liane

Loving Light Books

Available at:
Loving Light Books: www.lovinglightbooks.com
Amazon: www.amazon.com
Barnes & Noble: www.barnesandnoble.com

Also Available on Request at Local Bookstores

www.ingramcontent.com/pod-product-compliance
Lightning Source LLC
LaVergne TN
LVHW011242080426
835509LV00005B/594